PRO TACTICS™

PANFISH

WITHDRAWN

PRO TACTICS™ SERIES

PRO TACTICS™

PANFISH

Use the Secrets of the Pros to
Catch Bluegill, Crappie, and Perch

Jason Durham

THE LYONS PRESS
Guilford, Connecticut
An imprint of The Globe Pequot Press

The Lyons Press is an imprint of The Globe Pequot Press.
Pro Tactics is a trademark of Morris Book Publishing, LLC.

All interior photos by Jason Durham unless otherwise credited.

Text design by Peter Holm, Sterling Hill Productions

Library of Congress Cataloging-in-Publication Data is available.

ISBN 978-1-59921-277-7

Printed in the United States of America

10 9 8 7 6 5 4 3 2 1

CONTENTS

INTRODUCTION

Many of us found our angling beginnings at the end of a dock, watching a float bob in the waves as we waited for a fish—small in size but huge in emotional magnitude—to pull it under. A parent, grandparent, or caring individual stood nearby to guide the angling endeavors, hoping that a lifelong angler and outdoors steward would emerge. After swinging in countless panfish, gaining an appreciation for nature, and (one hopes) finding solace in even the worst outing, children often become hooked on fishing. This love for angling can grow as time passes.

But somewhere along the way, things generally change. Panfish are left to their own devices as the novice becomes increasingly knowledgeable, gradually redirecting his or her attention to the enthusiastic aerobatics of a bass, the fierce runs of the pike, and the thrill of landing a first walleye. Tackle boxes that were once sparsely decorated with bobbers, hooks, sinkers, and an old wooden hand-me-down plug now overflow with diversified equipment to catch bigger fish.

Countless people turn their backs on those angling roots to pursue larger gamefish—and don't look back. Yet if you speak to individuals who continue to predominantly pursue panfish, you'll find their dedication comparable to that of a muskie fisherman, often bordering on fanaticism. Armed with ultralight equipment in small boats that can reach the most remote waters, they come and go quietly, drawing little attention from others.

Most kids start their angling career with the ever-popular panfish species, and many never seem to outgrow the pursuit.

Whether you are a committed member of the panfish angler's somewhat secret society, an individual who sporadically indulges in an ice-fishing trip for perch, or someone who has sat on the edge of a pond swinging sunfish onto the bank, I wish you the best in discovering, or redefining, the art of catching panfish.

CHAPTER ONE

About Panfish

The term *panfish* is used somewhat loosely within angling circles, but it refers primarily to the Centrarchidae (sunfish) family. Many anglers consider only sunfish to be panfish, due to their pan-shaped body, and use the words interchangeably. Yet the species and geographic ranges vary, and all panfish are just as entertaining to catch, no matter what the classification. Because of their general eagerness to bite, all types of panfish can satisfy any angler, even with a short attention span, for hours. (And when the day concludes, they make wonderful table fare.)

To simplify the process of locating and persuading panfish, we'll examine three primary groups: sunfish, crappie, and perch. Although perch aren't a part of the Centrarchidae family, they are often associated with panfish because of their size, which is comparable to that of many panfish varieties, and rank as one of the more popular small fishes in North America.

The many sunfish varieties are, in many ways, the quintessential panfish. Plentiful and colorful, usually very cooperative, providing great sport, and tasty ... who could ask for more? DAWN PAPPAS

Opposite: The yellow perch is a staple in a great many locations and bites well throughout the calendar. Many anglers consider them the tastiest freshwater gamefish available. COREY STUDER

Sunfish

There are thirty species in the sunfish family, including but not limited to bluegill, pumpkinseed, rock bass, largemouth bass, and crappie. Most anglers call bluegills and pumpkinseeds "sunfish," and both of them are in fact considered to be "true" sunfish. All members of the sunfish family have rayed fins and a minimum of three anal fin spines. The sunfish family is native to North America, and member species reside only in fresh water from the Great Lakes to the Gulf of Mexico. They can be found in lakes, rivers, ponds, reservoirs, and streams, with eutrophic lakes having the greatest populations. These species enjoy being exposed to the sun, hence the name sunfish, but can often be found close to vegetation and brush that provide cover and security from larger predators such as northern pike, muskellunge, bass, and gar. Largemouth bass will often cohabitate with bluegill, pumpkinseed, and rock bass and will often swallow a small sunfish.

Perch

A handful of perch varieties exist, but the most commonly sought species is the yellow perch (*Perca flavescens*), more commonly referred to by anglers as simply "perch."

Belonging to the same family as walleye and sauger, perch are most popular throughout the Midwest and Great Lakes regions. Anglers targeting crappie and sunfish regularly run into perch and don't hesitate to bring home a mixed bag of the three.

Deeper, cool lakes with sprawling flats are primary locations for perch, but the availability of a strong and diverse forage base plays an important role in the production of larger fish. Bottom content dictates the

availability of varying food types: Rocks house crayfish, soft bottoms offer the necessary elements for insect hatches and livelihood of marine worms, and weeds provide refuge to numerous insect and invertebrate species. A large population of minnow varieties is another key element in finding lakes containing sizable perch. Numerous choices of forage types allow for less effort in feeding, a crucial component in growing large perch.

Perch congregate in schools and favor areas with gravel, rock, rubble, sand, and an array of vegetation. These schools travel close to the lake bottom and can be found even down to seventy feet. Steep drop-offs are additional prime territories for perch.

Perch are highly aggressive, sometimes scavenger-like, and are attracted to flash and vibration. Eager to bite a lure of much greater size than one might expect, perch are often caught while fishing for larger gamefish. They have relatively poor vision, making a strong case for using larger baits to provide more visual and auditory stimulus so that they can locate the presentation more easily. Daylight hours provide the greatest opportunities to catch perch due to their visual deficiencies after dark.

Crappie

The crappie, known in Louisiana and environs as "sac au lait," occurs in two varieties: black and white. JOHN JANOUSEK

There are two varieties of crappie: black and white. Black crappie typically reside in slightly deeper areas than white crappie, and the latter usually prefer warmer water. Many anglers fish for crappie due to the presence of large schools and their willingness to bite. Both varieties rank among the best freshwater fish to eat, which is one of the reasons anglers so willingly pursue these fish that rarely exceed two pounds. Although crappie won't give you a drag-peeling fight, they can sometimes be tricky to land due to the thin covering around their mouths, giving them the nickname "papermouth" and frustrating anglers who become overzealous when trying to land a large fish.

Crappie are anatomically designed for eating, with a slender body to cut through the water

easily, oversized eyes that can see a larger area and acutely discern edible targets, and a mouth that can expand into a cavernous opening, inhaling sustenance with little effort. The primary forage for crappie—minnows of differing varieties—plays a major role in fish location.

Crappies prefer numerous types of cover, including emergent and submergent brush in addition to natural and man-made formations. Conservation groups nationwide dedicate time and money to create log cribs and artificial structures, catering to the crappie's desire to make these places home while giving anglers more opportunity to catch this popular panfish.

Preferred Panfish Habitat

The natural habitats desired by crappie, bluegill, and perch vary slightly by species, but you'll find some striking similarities among them as well. The main factor prompting these species to choose cover is comfort: food, safety, and adequate oxygen levels. Since all three species are eagerly devoured by larger predators, cover is prime real estate. Emergent vegetation (weeds

Panfish prefer some types of habitat over others. Emergent vegetation is one favored area.

and plants that grow from the bottom of the lake and emerge above the surface), submergent vegetation (weeds and plants that stay beneath the water's surface), sticks, stumps, brush, and rock all play a role in panfish location. Fish taking residence in vegetation use the weeds for multiple purposes. Fish can hide in them to avoid predators; because some insects hatch from the vegetation, there's a food source present; and they can hide in the weeds to ambush passing schools of minnows.

Perch tend to favor the comfort of areas near rock, sand, and steep drop-offs where the bottom descends toward deeper water; they will relate to vegetation and other structural elements, too.

CHAPTER TWO

Getting Started

The basic equipment used for catching panfish is similar from one species to the next. It helps to understand the equipment's capabilities and to attain reasonably good skills in using it. Both may be achieved with some practice.

Many choices exist for each basic element of equipment. This book, sporting goods store employees, friends, and experts in the field can all offer you recommendations, but the one party that must ultimately find satisfaction with a selection is you. Whether a favorite rod or reel costs $5 or $5,000 doesn't matter as long as the equipment fulfills your needs.

Looking at the most basic equipment to some specialized items, the following recommendations provide good coverage for the various techniques you will need, and many of the situations you will face, while trying to catch sunfish, crappie, and perch.

Fishing Rods

Fishing rods are created from numerous materials and can be purchased in lengths of less than two feet, which would be common for ice fishing, up to about thirty feet, like some of the telescopic panfish rods used to strategically dunk a bait into the openings of vegetation without casting.

You don't need a second mortgage to get started fishing for panfish effectively; even a modest investment will afford you the tools you need.

These lengths are obviously at opposite ends of the rod-length spectrum, but each one plays a valuable role in catching panfish.

For individuals just getting started in fishing, and the majority of panfish applications, a rod between six and seven feet in length provides easy casting when combined with a good fishing reel. Rod length affects overall casting distance and offers the angler additional leverage when setting the hook. Generally speaking, the longer the rod, the longer the cast and the more leverage gained when setting the hook.

Some anglers choose length based upon storage space in the boat or what can fit inside a protective travel case. This is understandable and will work fine if the rod meets the owner's specifications for quality. A two-piece rod may be required for specific circumstances, but a one-piece design offers more sensitivity.

If trolling for crappie is your desire, then longer, more limber rods should be on the shopping list. Eight- to twelve-foot rods are appropriate for trolling and in some states multiple outfits can be used by one angler. Numerous lines in the water equate to better coverage of an area, more flexibility in bait presentation and experimentation, and greater odds for catching fish.

Action

The action of the rod refers to the way it flexes and bends from the tip along the blank. Rod actions are classified as extra fast, fast, moderate fast, moderate, and slow. An extra-fast-action rod is extremely sensitive but has less flexibility through the blank. This gives the angler great feeling when a fish bites, but it's easier for a fish to detect the fisherman as well. A slow-action rod bends along the entire blank and is common for trolling since it efficiently absorbs shock, keeping the lure in the fish's mouth instead of immediately tearing it out (which can occur with a faster-action rod). Moderate to fast rods are what most panfish anglers prefer, finding utility in the sensitive, yet flexible, tip.

As you try to determine which fishing rod to purchase, many people will provide their opinion as to which action works best for each species and under certain applications, but personal preference should determine which rod is best for you. General suggestions can be beneficial for someone who isn't familiar with rod action to avoid purchasing a "pool cue" or a "buggy whip," but some time should be devoted to finding a rod appropriately suited for your needs.

Since different rod manufacturers use varying techniques and materials in the construction of their products, comparing identical actions among a handful of rod companies will help you decide which one to purchase. Any angler would feel well prepared with fifty or sixty panfish rods of various length, action, and material leaning up against the wall of the garage, but for the majority of anglers this simply isn't feasible. Of course, if you take good care of your equipment, a rod can last many years. Much of the damage that fishing rods sustain takes place while they are stored in rod lockers and vehicles during travel. Line guides and reels can rub against the blank, causing scratches that not only affect the aesthetics of the rod but also create weak spots that may contribute to a broken piece of equipment. Sliding a protective sleeve over your fishing rods will protect them from abrasive contact, as well as prevent them from getting tangled up with one another.

Varieties

The two main varieties of rods used to catch panfish are casting and spinning. A casting rod provides a space for the reel on top of the reel seat, with the guides also positioned on top of the rod blank. A spinning rod is used with the reel positioned underneath the reel seat, with the guides also positioned beneath the rod blank. A casting rod can be used with a casting or spincasting reel (the latter is characterized by its enclosed spool of line), and a spinning rod can only be used with a spinning reel.

Casting Rods and Reels

A casting rod combined with a spincasting reel, called a spincast outfit, is definitely the easiest to use, especially for young kids.

Baitcast reels are another option to use on a casting rod. They appear different from a spincast reel, mainly because of the open spool design. Baitcast reels have a specific purpose and are generally used when casting larger baits with heavy line. They're not typically used to fish for panfish, since casting very small hooks and lures is difficult with a baitcast reel, but they can play a valuable role in trolling situations.

Spinning Rods and Reels

Spinning rod-and-reel combinations are very simple to use and can be mastered quickly by any angler. An important attribute of a spinning reel is a drag system that allows fish to strip line before tension causes it to break. You might not think this is very important in the quest for panfish, but many times a larger gamefish is hooked even though that might not be the intent. A large fish can be landed on very light line with a correctly operating and properly adjusted drag.

Setting the drag can be accomplished by fixing the end of your fishing line to the end of a solid, stationary object, then lifting the rod to make it load up (which means the rod is at its maximum bend). At this point the line should smoothly peel from the spool. Simply giving the line a quick yank directly from the reel spool won't accurately set the drag and can result in a broken line and lost fish.

Fly Rods

Another popular rod-and-reel combination for panfish is the fly rod. Also commonly used for trout, a fly rod can cast a hook of nearly nonexistent weight. Many anglers enjoy the challenge of mastering the technique required to cast a fly rod, which differs greatly from that of a spinning, spincasting, or baitcasting outfit. The forward-and-back motion while

Opposite: Spincast rods are so easy to use that even a young child can proficiently learn the technique for casting.

simultaneously stripping line from the reel takes some coordination, but fighting a fish with a fly rod, even a small bluegill, is quite enjoyable.

Line

Line strength is calculated by its tested breaking point, typically measured in pounds. For instance, a line that breaks under a minimum of six pounds of pressure has the tensile strength labeled as six-pound test, although it could actually be slightly stronger than the label states. With a properly adjusted drag, it's possible to land a fish much larger than six pounds on six-pound test, but the opposite also holds true. A fish much smaller than six pounds could break the same line if there is more than six pounds of pressure exerted on the line, which commonly occurs when an angler gets overzealous in pulling back on the fishing rod, a practice that's sometimes hard to avoid in the excitement of hooking a nice fish. Line wear and decomposition are other factors contributing to line failure.

There are several attributes of fishing line that should be taken into consideration when determining which one to purchase. The first is the material of which the fishing line is composed. Monofilament, braid, copolymer, and fluorocarbon are all available, although different manufacturers construct each type with varying techniques and formulas. Other factors include color, diameter, and price.

Monofilament is the most common type of fishing line and is constructed by extruding heated polymers to create a single strand of material. Although monofilament is often clear in appearance, it can also be found in translucent hues of green, blue, yellow, red, brown, and even photochromic—a property that allows the line to change colors in direct sunlight, increasing visibility for the angler.

The color of fishing line should be considered, yet clear remains the most popular choice for all situations. Matching line color to the background color of the underwater environment creates a camouflage effect, hiding the line. In very weedy conditions a green or brown line might be considered. Some brightly colored fishing lines can simplify use by the angler, especially when tying knots or attempting to detect light bites by watching the line, but will be much more easily seen by fish. This is a compromise some anglers are willing to make, especially when it comes to threading the eye of a hook with a thin-diameter line.

Braided line is created by braiding numerous individual strands of material. This can produce a line with superior strength, ultrathin diameter, and zero stretch, thus giving it the common classification as "superline." With these qualities, you might wonder why anyone would choose another type of line. Superlines do have some great qualities, but there are a couple of characteristics that should be considered. First, since the line has no stretch, a hard hookset by the angler can tear a fish's mouth or straighten a hook, so some precaution must be taken. Because braided line is so strong, it can also cause additional wear to lesser quality line guides. Braided line is opaque, so even though the diameter of braid is much less than that in the corresponding strength of monofilament, the fish cannot see through it—a good reason to selectively match the line color to the available underwater background colors.

The price of braided line is much more than monofilament, but when you look at the cost over time, it's nearly identical. Superlines don't develop memory or deteriorate as fast and can therefore last for years.

Fluorocarbon line was originally developed to be used in ultraclear salt water, but it has become increasingly popular for freshwater applications. This line has nearly the same light refraction properties as water and performs much like a monofilament line. However, fluorocarbon does not absorb water, making it important to keep the line wet while tying a knot. Some anglers actually cinch the knot while holding it underwater to help reduce friction, creating a strong, secure bond between the lure and line.

Knots

While endless knot configurations exist, there are two that every angler should know and become proficient in tying. The improved clinch knot is a popular fishing knot and works great with monofilament lines.

The Palomar knot is ranked as one of the strongest known and is a good choice for braid, fluorocarbon, and monofilament. But whichever line you use, and no matter what knot you choose, a fishing line's nemesis is friction. Heat that's generated while cinching any knot can damage and compromise its integrity, contributing to the likelihood of losing a nice fish or an expensive lure. To keep friction to a minimum, use water or saliva to lubricate your fishing line as you tighten the knot.

Terminal Tackle

An intimidating aspect of any fishing outing is determining what terminal tackle is needed. To simplify this process, first determine your angling destination, then collect information from knowledgeable sources such as fishing guides, local experts, and bait shop employees to decide what you need to buy at the tackle shop and what you already own.

When thinking about putting together tackle for panfish, lean toward items that are very small in size. What's small? Well, on average a crappie has a mouth slightly larger than a quarter, a perch can fit a nickel in its maw, and many bluegill can only get a dime between their jaws.

Many anglers use hooks, jigs, and lures that are much too large for the majority of panfish, whose primary food sources include insects, small minnows, and zooplankton. The angler's goal is to match the natural food that is currently present in each particular body of water and use equipment suited for those forage varieties' sizes.

The primary tackle you'll need to catch panfish are hooks, jigheads, soft plastic bodies, floats, and weights. A few other options include small floating, diving, or sinking lures, including spinners. Though it sounds simple, these pieces of tackle are offered in thousands of varieties. The following list will help by giving an overview of what should fill your tackle box.

The Well-Equipped Tackle Box

Small Live-Bait and Aberdeen Hooks (sizes 4, 6, 8, 10, 12)

Some tackle shops have hook displays that seem to span a city block. There appears to be a hook for practically any situation, with specialized designs, space-age sharpening processes, and labels that scream at the consumer, touting much more than simply "fishhooks." As with any type of tackle, a little bit of knowledge and an educated focus on size and performance, rather than packaging alone, will lead you to the right selection. Some companies use identical packaging formats for different products, often displaying text that classifies it as useful for "bass, pike, trout, and panfish." Don't automatically assume that a package labeled as proper for "panfish" will fit your application. Tackle manufacturers routinely do this to broaden the anticipated return on investment from the consumer. If you can purchase one bait or hook that can be used for five different species, then why buy five different species-exclusive items? Looking specifically at hooks for panfish, a couple of designs will provide the most worthwhile.

Conversely, packages that state application for a species other than panfish may also work well to catch crappie, perch, and sunfish. A favorite example is the salmon-egg hook. Automatically assuming that a salmon-egg hook is strictly for trout or salmon will find you passing up a great style of hook for live-bait presentation to catch panfish.

For panfish, two styles can cover nearly every situation. The first, an Aberdeen hook, has a long shank that makes hook removal easier, especially for aggressive sunfish that can take a hook deeply. The second style, live-bait hooks, includes a few more designs, including bait-holder and the aforementioned salmon-egg hooks. Bait-holder (and often salmon-egg) hooks have one or two barbs that protrude from the back of the shank, keeping live bait like leeches and worms from sliding down to the bend and more efficiently hiding the majority of the hook.

The smallest live-bait hooks commonly displayed in tackle shop sections for walleye are also good crossover selections. Look for hooks constructed of the lightest wire, and choose quality name brands to ensure integrity. Gold, nickel, and bronze are no longer the only hook color options; hues vary from subtle green to intensely contrasting pink, red, orange, chartreuse, and white.

Assorted Split-Shot and Bell Sinkers

Because split shot are attached to the line without retying, they can accompany just about any type of presentation requiring a weight adjustment. Assortment packs containing various sizes offer the angler flexibility in weighting options and are one of the least expensive items to purchase for angling.

Both drop-shot and dropper rigs utilize bell sinkers, a great weight for making contact with the bottom. Sizes from $\frac{1}{8}$ ounce up to 1 $\frac{1}{2}$ ounces will cover everything from shallow water to deep, as well as situations involving current.

Thill Balsa Floats (spring and slip types)

The Achilles heel of any float is water, particularly if moisture penetrates the interior and causes the bobber to sink. Thill floats won't take on water because of a solid balsa-wood core that won't shatter when an awkward cast causes it to careens into a rock, or if it drops to the bottom of the boat. Simply stated, balsa trumps plastic.

Spring bobbers are clipped to the line by means of (you guessed it) a spring, while a slip float is threaded onto the line and combined with a bobber stop, which is simply a bead and small thread.

The practicality of using a slip or spring bobber depends partially on how deep you want your bait to sit in relation to the overall depth of the water. A spring bobber is attached in a fixed position, and the entire length of line to the bait achieves the desired presentation depth. That's easy enough if you're only fishing in two feet of water, but if you want your bait down seven feet below the float, making an accurate cast with seven feet of line hanging from the end of your rod can be tricky, not to mention dangerous if there are others nearby. Even though a spring bobber is quick and convenient, deepwater applications call for a slip float.

Of the two available designs, spring bobbers are the simplest to attach and remove, making them the choice of convenience. Yet slip bobbers perform slightly better, in part because the line smoothly slides through the center, eliminating potential wear at the point of attachment that could otherwise result in a broken line with a spring float. Thill's Pro Series of floats has a grommet built into the stem of the slip bobber, reducing friction when the line slides through its center.

The theme of downsizing for panfish continues when selecting a float. Smaller is better, but visibility can become an issue. One option to aid visual location is a float with a protruding thin wire affixed to its top. This sticks up higher above the surface, which is especially important when the float has been properly "shotted," a weighting method that renders the float nearly neutrally buoyant.

Slip Bobber Stops

If you're going to use slip bobbers, you're going to need slip bobber stops. The most popular ones are a simple thread knot, with a bead tied to the main fishing line at the maximum point to which the float should rise. If,

for example, you would like your bait suspended below the float at six feet, the bobber stop would be tied on six feet from the bait.

A brightly colored bobber stop allows the angler to visually pinpoint whether the bait has descended to its resting position below the float. If the line stops flowing through the slip bobber, more weight will need to be added at the end of your line.

One problem encountered when using a slip bobber is that if your line should break, either on a fish or in brush (which is common during spring), the slip bobber slides off the now-bare end of your fishing line and rests on the surface until you retrieve it. A simple cure for this is to attach another bobber stop a couple of feet above your hook, beneath the bobber. This way, if your line breaks near the hook, which is a high-percentage area of line failure, the float will come aboard along with your line, allowing you to maintain your current boat position.

Lindy Rig Components (hook, swivel, walking sinker)

Historically respected as one of the most productive walleye presentations of all time, the Lindy Rig can be adapted for catching virtually any species. Bottom-relating fish are most likely to fall prey to the natural appearance of a Lindy Rig, although small floats or a floating hook can be added to raise the bait above the bottom. Perch and sunfish are commonly caught using a Lindy Rig, while encounters with crappie are less frequent.

The Lindy Rig was developed decades ago and features a small walking sinker that easily slides along the bottom; a swivel that prevents line twist and keeps the sinker separate from the hook; a length of fishing line called the snell, or leader, which is commonly twenty to sixty inches in length, and a single, plain, live-bait hook tipped with a minnow, leech, nightcrawler, or any other type of live bait. The Lindy Rig permits the live bait to swim quite freely while in close proximity to the bottom. The walking sinker remains in contact with the bottom as the presentation is slowly dragged using a trolling motor at a very low speed, or as the angler slow pulls the fishing rod after a substantial cast, letting the Lindy Rig rest motionless on the bottom for a few seconds while retrieving a few inches of slack, then repeating. The beauty of the Lindy Rig is its ability to let line flow freely through the sinker without resistance when a fish grabs the bait.

Lindy Rigs can be purchased as a kit containing the hook, monofilament leader, swivel, and walking sinker preassembled to conveniently tie on and fish. The components can also be purchased separately, allowing the angler to fine-tune the rig by choosing the desired line weight, leader length, hook size, and walking sinker weight. Beads, spinners, and floats can also be added to attract panfish.

Jigheads of Various Colors and Shapes (³⁄₁₆, ¹⁄₁₆, ¹⁄₃₂, and ¹⁄₆₄ ounce)

Practically every shape imaginable has been adapted for the head design of a jig. Even so, ten years from now there might be another handful of options. The most popular jig design is the standard ball-head, which is available with or without a barbed collar. If you are threading a soft plastic body onto a jighead, the barbed collar will keep it snug to the head, preventing it from sliding down the hook shank. The ball-head jig is a good all-purpose shape, and a number of weight and color options should be on hand for any fishing trip.

Other available designs include darter heads, aspirin heads, bullet heads, shad darts, stand-up heads, mushroom heads, and tube jigheads. Each one has a specific purpose relating to the manner in which it moves through the water or lies on the bottom. Experiment with various designs for unique actions, stocking up on those you find particularly useful.

Dressed jigheads are another option, and they vary from marabou feathers to natural or synthetic hair. Out of the water, a hand-tied marabou jig is soft to the touch, while hair is coarse. The marabou jig is a good leech and insect imitator, especially in hues of brown and black, while the hair jig's tantalizing movement draws attention from all species of panfish. (A chunk of live bait or Berkley Power Bait Micros adds flavor to the offering, causing panfish to hold on to the jig longer.)

The majority of the jigs in a panfish box should be very light, ¹⁄₆₄ to ¹⁄₁₆ ounce, while a handful of slightly heavier jigs provide greater flexibility in wind and current. But caution should be exercised before purchasing a jighead based solely upon its weight. This is especially important when ordering jigheads from an online or mail-order store. Weight won't matter if the species you're after can't fit the hook in its mouth; small hook sizes are a necessity for panfish.

The color of a jighead can be important—especially when fish are not feeding actively—and should be chosen carefully, taking water clarity into consideration. Fish have rods and cones in their eyes to evaluate both

Jigs are among the most effective bait that can be used for panfish and a variety of other fish. Feather jigs, pictured here, are but one variant.

light and color, but scientists agree that fish perceive colors differently than humans do. Over the years anglers have discovered certain colors and combinations that seem to perform consistently under specific conditions. These color preferences often vary from lake to lake, since water clarity, background coloration (weeds, sand, etc.), and available food have an impact on what shades are most productive. Generally speaking, bright colors work well in dirty water, while natural colors do a better job in clear water. Of course, fishing would be overly simplified if this always held true, so it is important to experiment.

Miniature Teardrops, Ants, and Other Ice-fishing Jigs (for finicky fish)

Tiny ice-fishing jigs are perfect for crappie, perch, and sunfish that snub other presentations. Early spring is an obvious period for these baits, but be sure to use correspondingly sized live bait or plastic trailers. Large products hung from a tiny ice jig impede the hook from penetrating the fish's mouth and negate the idea of persuading apprehensive fish by downsizing.

If you ice fish on a regular basis, you can simply throw your ice-fishing tackle box inside your larger, open-water box. Remember, if you choose an extremely small bait, you'll want a small float as well.

Soft Plastic Bodies (two inches and less in length)

If it's alive, there's probably a soft plastic bait on the market to replicate the shape. Crickets, crayfish, minnows, flies, frogs, even ducks are made into soft plastic baits for fishing (although I don't recommend using the latter for panfish, even if it's flavor enhanced). Soft plastic baits with profiles similar to available forage produce well, and some additional designs that look like they emerged from a horror movie can turn passive fish into a feeding horde. Two of the most popular soft plastic baits of all time, the tube bait and the curly-tail grub, are deadly on crappie, sunfish, and perch. Select a few styles to start, but be sure to buy a variety of colors in each soft plastic design. Lean toward baits fortified with scent and flavor, like Berkley's Power Bait line.

It should be noted that soft plastic baits grouped together in a tackle box can quickly turn into a gooey mess, especially if the product comes into contact with a painted lure or other soft baits made from different types of plastic or chemicals. The reaction won't cause your tackle box to burst into flames, but it can result in permanent damage to the storage container and decomposition of tackle. Soft-sided organizers that use plastic bags to contain different baits won't allow unwanted contact and will additionally protect them from harmful moisture that, over time, can cause discoloration and swelling of the artificial bodies.

Gulp!

Similar in design to soft plastic baits, Berkley Gulp! is composed of all-natural scents and flavors that "bleed" into the water, dispersing more attractant than plastic baits. Gulp! can go head to head with live bait and is a great choice in the hot summer months when keeping minnows, worms, and leeches alive can be a challenge. The product line's maggots, earthworms, minnows, and leeches are all hot baits for panfish and should be a staple in your tackle box.

The products come in a resealable bag, identical to those used for

plastic baits; but unlike plastic bodies, Gulp! baits can dry out and become stiff within a few hours, so it's imperative to seal the package tightly. Once you're finished fishing for the day, they should be removed from the hook to prevent shrinkage that will make them difficult to remove later on. If you've never used a Berkley Gulp! before, give it try. You'll be impressed with its fish-catching ability.

Opposite: A crankbait fooled this nice specimen into taking it. Crankbaits can be used to probe a wide variety of depths.
NICK PAPPAS

Small Floating and Sinking Crankbaits (three inches or less)

Small crankbaits can be cast or trolled effectively. The body design of a miniature crankbait has to be small enough for a panfish to consider it edible and must also have hooks that can fit into the fish's mouth.

A crappie has a greater tolerance for larger crankbaits than a bluegill does. Both crappie and perch will attack crankbaits up to three inches at

Crankbaits come in a variety of sizes, shapes, colors, and lip sizes, which determine diving depth.

The Hornet is available in both floating and sinking models in natural colors, in addition to a couple with more attention-grabbing finishes.

times, but you're better off starting with lures half that size. Due to their miniscule size and equally small lips, panfish crankbaits won't dive very deep. This isn't a problem if the fish are positioned close to the surface, but when fish are located near the bottom—common for perch—the crankbait won't make it to the strike zone unless either of two things changes. Weight must be added to the crankbait, which often impedes its action, or a switch can be made to an accurately weighted, sinking crankbait that can be worked along the bottom after its descent.

The #3 Hornet, a 1⅜-inch crankbait created by Polish manufacturer Salmo, is a favorite of anglers worldwide. The small overall size and tapered body make it easy for any panfish to grab, and the single rear treble hook balances the bait nicely. The Hornet is available in both floating and sinking models in natural colors, in addition to a couple with more attention-grabbing finishes.

The greatest challenge in finding crankbaits that are applicable for panfish isn't locating the proper size, but rather purchasing a small crankbait that runs "true" right from the box. Because of their size, tiny crankbaits are more susceptible to influences from line diameter and retrieval speed, two factors that are easily remedied. On the other hand, poorly constructed crankbaits simply cannot be fixed. A crooked lip or twisted body takes more than a pair of pliers to fix; it takes a replacement lure.

Spinners (hinge spinners, in-line spinners, and small spinnerbaits)

Because of their combined vibration and visual flash, spinners remain at the forefront of panfish baits. Hinge spinners (those that can be attached to your weighted jighead of choice) essentially create a miniature spinnerbait and offer the flexibility of choosing the weight, body type, and spinner color and size. Further, those attributes can be changed at any time, making for a highly adaptive lure.

Small spinnerbaits are similar in concept but are a one-piece design. The decision of blade type, color, and size, as well as skirt color and weight, must be decided upon in the tackle aisle.

In-line spinners come in two varieties: the one-piece design like a spinnerbait and the interchangeable design, akin to a hinge spinner. One-piece inline spinners are classic lures that have familiar old names like Mepps and Panther Martin. Commonly associated with trout and smallmouth bass, these have been catching panfish both intentionally and inadvertently for decades.

Little Joe's True-Spin in-line spinner can be attached directly to a jig or small spoon, and can supplement a crankbait using a clasp or split ring. The light wire provides flexibility for premium amplification of sound and vibration, while the main attached bait provides the bulk.

All of these spinner types effectively imitate the flash of an injured minnow, reflecting light with each thump of the blade and are especially valuable for catching active crappie and perch.

Additional Essentials

Other suggested items to include in a well-equipped tackle box are line clippers, a stringer if you plan to keep fish, Lindy fish-handler gloves (for those inevitable encounters with larger, toothy predators that stalk panfish), a small forceps or hook-out, a camera (for catch-and-release photos), and a Gerber or similar multitool (for inevitable technical difficulties).

Put That Leader Down

Many items collect in the tackle-box trays over the years, and it becomes difficult to part with any of those objects, as they all seem potentially valuable. Nobody enjoys losing tackle due to a misjudged cast, unexpected theft, corrosion, or aggressive battle with a fish. We can eliminate or reduce some of these, such as locking compartments and garages to deter theft, frequently changing line to ensure integrity, or double-checking knots for solidity.

Certain choices, however, such as using a wire leader, may provide tackle security but can also negatively influence fish behavior.

Sunfish in many lakes are so plentiful that the use of a leader or snap swivel shouldn't matter, right? Considering that the stiff wire leader will first limit the action of your bait, then restrict its flexibility when a fish attempts to grab it and swim away, you're better off leaving the leader in your tackle box. Even though some of the smaller fish and an occasional keeper will be caught, your catch rate and average size will greatly increase without the cumbersome leader.

Size Matters

Softball-size bobbers, monster hooks, and thick-diameter line are three factors that will immediately affect the number of panfish you catch, and not in a positive manner. Panfish are not a "one size fits all" species. It is critical to size each component relative both to the target fish and to one another. For example, let's say that you have an ideally sized, hackled ant tied on four-pound-test line to present for wary spring sunfish but are using an oversize, round plastic bobber with it. This float will cause excessive and unnecessary disruption, spooking the cautious early-season inhabitants. Additionally, the resistance caused by the overly buoyant float won't allow it to gently slip beneath the surface as it should, and now the aggravated fish cannot swim away easily. If the fish does muster the strength to sink this huge float, another issue arises. The pressure applied during the hookset is now absorbed by the submerged bobber, resulting in failure to drive the hook through the fish's mouth. Going the extra mile to find the right-size float only makes sense.

Let's take a moment to consider the line you're using. The panfish we seek are not huge, and line testing between two and six pounds will serve well. Such line has the additional advantages of being difficult for the fish to detect, easy to knot, and retaining good flexibility, which helps with lure action. To maximize these properties, it is also beneficial to change line on a regular basis—serious anglers do so at least once a year—to maintain the line's integrity and avoid excessive memory (characterized by loops that stay in the line as it comes off the spool).

Imagine that you simply didn't have time to respool before the first spring outing. Your rod and reel may have sat idle for an extended period of time, perhaps months. Casting distance will be compromised due to the heavily coiled line, and detecting a bite will be equally difficult, since a fish must swim farther or shake your bait even harder to alert you through the spirals of shock-absorbing line.

The third component that requires close attention when determining proper size is the hook. It could be said that this is the most important component of any presentation. Tying on a huge hook, and thinking that simply covering it with gobs of bait will catch fish, won't perform with any realistic hope of satisfaction. You'll get plenty of bites, nearly every one of them resulting in a bare hook and no fish to show for it. Lean toward hooks that are smaller than what you think would be practical. With panfish it's very improbable that the hook you choose is too small. You may need a small pair of forceps to remove the hook from time to time, but you're going to get more bites and hook more fish than if you chose a hook that's even slightly larger than the needs at hand. Remember, some of the natural food panfish eat are miniscule organisms that are much smaller than any panfish jig available.

CHAPTER THREE

Crappie through the Seasons

Even when available in healthy numbers in a given lake, river, or reservoir, crappie won't be found in every cubic foot of water. Depending on the size of the lake, there might not even be a crappie in every square surface mile. Fortunately they're predisposed to schooling, and when one crappie is located, a number of fish are often nearby. Understanding the seasonal movements of crappie will not only help you find active fish but also will aid in eliminating unproductive water.

Spring Crappie

During the early part of spring, crappies venture into shallow backwater coves to engage in a short but intense feeding binge. In the northern portion of the nation, this may be only a day or two after the ice has melted from lakes. The difficulty lies in finding which specific shallow-water areas are holding fish. Simply positioning your boat in a couple feet of water

Here's a satisfied angler with a nice one. Many anglers end up specializing in this species and never look back.

and casting haphazardly will rarely work. Small, shallow bays and arms that have a dark, muddy bottom that warms quickly under a sunny spring sky, in addition to brush and last year's standing vegetation, tend to hold greater populations of crappie. Once you discover one of these areas, it's typical to find crappie in the same spot annually, as they commonly spawn repeatedly in the same general vicinity.

Professional angler Ron Anlauf shares a similar formula for locating early-season crappie, suggesting the exploration of slightly deeper depressions within these smaller bays.

"If the water's clear and calm enough, you'll be able to see the depression (and the fish); otherwise you'll have to rely on electronics to do your investigating," he suggests. "A likely hot spot would include a two- or three-foot deeper pocket surrounded by approximately four to eight feet of water. Throw in some green weeds for cover, and you may have found a real honey hole."

Understanding post-ice-out locations remains important. The fish will move in and out of these shallow water areas a couple of times before spawning and then finally exiting until the following year. An angler can extend the period of quality crappie fishing by expanding the area of interest by a few hundred yards. Since we already know that the fish return to a certain backbay every year, those fish will swim in and out of the area, staging at medial depths outside the spawning bay, as Anlauf points out.

These fish are not floating about aimlessly, as one might believe. Prior to spawning, the fish eat voraciously to prepare their bodies for the stress experienced over the following six to eight days. After the spawn, crappies congregate and again find refuge in close proximity to the spawning area but are either recovering in a semi-lethargic state or actively feeding—two differing attitudes to consider when choosing an appropriate presentation.

Techniques for Prespawn Crappie

A favorite technique for spring crappie is to suspend a miniature jig with an energetic minnow below a small balsa float. Since the crappie will be quite lethargic because of the cooler water, smaller presentations are better.

A minnow beneath a float is an excellent technique to catch monster crappie all year long, but the minnow should be hooked in a manner that allows it to swim freely in an attitude parallel to the bottom. When you use a float and a standard live-bait hook, the minnow should be carefully hooked through the back. If the baitfish is hooked along the back closer to the head, it will usually swim with its head up. Positioning the hook closer to the tail angles the minnow downward, causing it to swim toward the bottom. A minnow hooked toward the front, or at least the middle, will swim in a larger area because it has the ability to propel itself toward the surface with less resistance than swimming downward against the float.

A different option includes a jig with a ninety-degree bend in the hook, so that the shank lays parallel to the bottom, and requiring the minnow to be hooked through the lips to give it a natural, horizontal appearance.

Since crappie can be apprehensive during the early part of spring, the combination of a balsa float and jig/minnow works well due to the fact that the bait isn't moving quickly through a great amount of water. Even though the minnow is swimming naturally, it's moving very little horizontally. It tends to stay suspended yet continually active. This allows a wary crappie plenty of time to make the decision to engulf it.

Whether you choose to use a weighted jig or a plain live-bait hook in combination with one or two split shot is primarily a matter of personal preference. The use of a jighead gives an opportunity to display a small bit of color, which may or may not affect the fish in a positive manner, depending entirely on the prevailing mood of the prespawn crappie.

It is unlikely that you will need slip bobbers in many of these situations. Since we're talking about prespawn crappie that inhabit shallow water, these deepwater floats won't be necessary. Just a couple of feet is typically all the distance you'll need under the float.

Spawning Crappie

The spawning period can be when crappie anglers catch some of the biggest fish of the year, and a time when crappies are more susceptible to overharvest, since they are congregated in small, shallow bays. As water temperatures reach fifty-seven to sixty-four degrees, male crappie move into shallow spawning areas, but water temperature isn't the sole determiner for initiating the start of the spawn.

"Consistent weather and steady water temps are critical for finding the largest numbers of fish up shallow, and when they'll be the most active,"

states Anlauf. "Severe cold fronts can shut the whole thing down, at least for the short term, and are something to be aware of."

Prompted by favorable environmental conditions, the male begins creating the nest—a small circle approximately one foot in diameter—which he fashions by fanning the bottom with his tail. Soon larger female crappie will join the males, and together they combine eggs and milt in the water. The female produces up to 150,000 eggs, dispersing a portion or the entirety, then leaves the parenting to the male, who stays with the young until they hatch and can leave the nest on their own. Predators such as bluegill, perch, bullheads, and salamanders all willingly eat crappie eggs, but the male is dedicated to providing protection. The eggs hatch in approximately seven days. When crappie fry emerge from the egg, they first feed on zooplankton, which makes up their diet for the first year, and then graduate to minnows, a primary food source from that period forward.

To help sustain current populations, anglers should avoid keeping too many spawning crappie. Since crappie lay a large number of eggs and reproduce quite quickly, putting a few in the live well won't be detrimental to the fishery. However, since the fish are relegated to small areas where spawning takes place (and remain highly committed to the nest, attacking an accurately placed bait), they are very susceptible to overharvest. Take a conservative approach, and protect our resources for the future.

Spawning Crappie Techniques

Since spawning crappie remain so committed to their nest, an effective presentation is one that allows the bait to remain on or over the nest. A good choice, and one that is quite popular for spawning crappie, is the same presentation that caught so many prespawn fish: a jig/minnow and float combination. But there's another option that at times will outperform and outcatch the traditional jig/minnow and float.

Opposite: This angler knows live bait can be one of the best ways to entice crappie to come your way this time of year.
JOHN JANOUSEK

There's nothing like the heft of a good crappie to help chase away the chill of an early-season outing.

35

Using a bobber and jig only works well when adjusted to the proper depth. Spawning crappie linger fairly close to the bottom and move vertically just a couple of feet, even less horizontally unless seriously threatened. If you've set your float to a depth of four feet and you're fishing in six feet of water, you're going to be just fine and catch a good bunch of fish. But typically the contour of the lake bottom rises and descends, as opposed to remaining completely flat. When you cast the jig/minnow and float, the minnow hits the water and slowly descends from the surface to the maximum depth that the bobber will allow. Any fish that swims below that point must rise to eat the minnow, and if the bait is too high, the fish simply won't bite.

One answer to this is the drop-shot rig. This presentation was originally used in western reservoirs and Japan to catch bass in superclear, highly pressured waters. The system consists of a weight attached to the end of your fishing line and a small hook attached six to twenty-four inches above the weight. For spawning crappie, a length of six to ten inches of line between the weight and hook is ideal. To create a drop-shot rig, you must first tie on the hook using a Palomar knot, leaving a long tag end where the weight will be attached. A small live-bait hook is just the right size for a small minnow, or soft plastic bait of a couple inches. Now tie a weight, ¼ to ½ ounce, to the free end of the fishing line, and you're set to go.

The philosophy behind the drop-shot rig is that the weight makes contact with the bottom, and the hook, with either a soft plastic body or live bait attached, will descend afterward. As both items lie on the bottom, the angler gently raises the rod to lift the hook from the bottom but is careful not to move the weight.

Now the rod tip can be twitched and dropped to make the baited hook dance, shake, rise, and fall without moving the bait from the nest of the aggressive crappie. In essence, the drop-shot rig is a marionette, with the angler acting as puppeteer. This rise and fall to the bottom looks threatening, as if the susceptible eggs are being attacked, prompting the protective crappie to take action.

The drop-shot rig is a great tool for fooling big crappie. The technique may have been originated for bass fishing, but its effectiveness for crappie, as shown, is superb. KELLEY CIRKS

Postspawn Crappie

The period immediately following spawning can be one of unpredictability for an angler. Some fish will feed voraciously, while others will be in a state of recovery and very sedate. After exiting the shallow spawning bays, crappie take up position just outside these coves for several days before moving into their early-summer locations. At this point the crappie begin to school up and move together.

Postspawn Crappie Techniques

A slip-bobber and jig/minnow combination will produce for the fish that remain fairly aggressive, but those that are tired from the spawn may not seem interested. If you see fish present that are easily spooked, try downsizing the presentation and using longer casts. A tiny ice-fishing jig with a single waxworm won't cast very far, but pair it with a float while using a long fishing rod and large-spooled reel to extend your casting distance, and you'll make fewer fish scatter.

Postspawn crappie begin to make short migrations from their spawning areas toward larger, main lake haunts. Areas of the lake that form a bottleneck, where the shoreline converges to create a smaller passageway, can be literal fish highways as crappie move through backwater channels. Often these areas have small bridges and some degree of current.

Early-Summer Crappie

During the early summer period, crappie remain in shallow to medium depths of just a foot or two of water, out to about twelve feet, especially as these depths relate to main lake structure. The fish at this point will be roaming, searching for food, and establishing residence in an area for a few days when larger food sources are found and weather conditions remain stable. At this point, cover plays a major role in their location. Large, green, leafy weeds that provide cover, house minnows, provide hatching areas for insects, and produce oxygen are often the preferred location. Brush, sticks,

Wading can be among the most effective means of reaching shallow-water crappie, as well as other panfish.

PLAYING THE WADING GAME

All freshwater fish utilize shallow water at some time in their lives. The migration to shallow water accompanies spring's warmer temperatures and eventually progresses into the spawn. Canals, small bays, and hidden backwater that warm quickly often accommodate a variety of fish species, and many will continue to utilize those shallow water areas throughout the season, especially if there is adjacent current. Small, shallow lakes that become weed choked and uninviting by July are at the top of the list during the early part of the season, since getting a boat into some of these hotspots can be more of a challenge than the fishing is worth. Because the water may be only inches deep and often silt laden, your best choice may be to leave the boat at home.

Stealth Stalking

Shore fishing is always an option, but why limit yourself to open casting areas? Waders give you flexibility where shore fishing does not. A good pair of waders will allow you to venture into the nooks where fish like to hide, seeking out comfortable areas and stalking prey in the process. Since shallow-water fish can be easily spooked, keeping a low profile is often necessary to catch numbers of fish. Waders give anglers the opportunity to sneak effectively through shallow water, since the angler's body is positioned closer to the surface, compared to sitting in a boat, and casts less of a shadow than watercraft.

Take Aim

In general, anglers should cast toward one of two types of structures: emergent and submergent. Emergent structures include any vegetation, sticks, trees, and the like that protrude out of the water. Submergent structures include weeds, logs, and even old tires that are located underneath the surface of the water.

When an angler casts from shore, trees, brush, and the possibility of wet feet all restrict his or her ability to hit highly productive areas from various angles. Waders grant the opportunity for casts to reach areas untouchable from shore, due to fewer obstructions and increased ability to target both kinds of structure.

Safety

Since waders enable greater shallow-water mobility, it's easy to become overly secure with their potential. Insulated waders keep you dry, resist loss of body heat, and do not restrict movement. However, you are not invincible simply because you are wearing them. Stepping into unknown deep water will fill waders quickly, and if you're far from your vehicle, a long, cold walk will be in your future. Carry a long stick to test the bottom before you step off a ledge or into a silt-filled hole, and beware of areas with strong current. Cautious anglers are just as concerned about getting home safely as they are about getting fish.

Once spawning is complete, crappie hang around shallow water areas for a short period, then move on to deeper refuge.
BILL LINDNER

and outside edges of pencil reeds that grow close to deeper water are also good places to look.

Sweetening your small artificial with something edible like a waxworm can make all the difference to the fish you want to attract.

Early-Summer Crappie Techniques

Since the crappie are actively searching and feeding, now is a good time to use a presentation that covers more water. Instead of soaking a minnow below a float, try a jighead with a small minnow, but leave the float in the tackle box. A 1/32-ounce jighead is a good size, and the minnow should be delicately hooked through the lips. So hooked, the minnow can be cast and slowly retrieved, remaining parallel to the bottom with a natural appearance. As the fish become increasingly active, artificial soft baits and hair jigs begin to catch just as many fish as their live-bait cohorts.

Mid- to Late-Summer Crappie

When summer rolls around, many lakes favor the boater in finding good crappie locations.

Warming water temperatures now bring schools of crappie to deeper water. Though sparsely scattered fish may still be caught along the inside weed edges and shallow cover, a large number of the fish move out to ten feet of water or more and hold on weed lines, flooded timber along creek channels, humps composed of either weed or rock, and areas with current. These structures serve a specific purpose besides providing a sense of security for the fish: They act as boundaries for cornering baitfish. Regularly situated in the upper portion of the water column, crappie typically dwell toward the top fifteen feet.

During low-light periods like early morning and evening, crappie can be seen breaking the surface with their dorsal fins or the "smuck" of

The warmth of a July afternoon prompts an occasional swim from a paddleboat, but don't forget your fishing gear—crappie action heats up too!

During high-activity periods, take the water's clarity and turbidity into account to determine when to fish a given body of water.

their lips. Bodies of water with diminished water clarity have a period of intense activity that is less prominent compared to lakes with clear water.

Deep schools of crappie locate themselves in proximity to structure, not necessarily mimicking the movements of the wandering bait schools. Smaller, loosely scattered schools of crappie move closer to structure when forage dissipates and between low-light periods.

Finding these deepwater schools can take time, and without some good-quality marine electronics, the task will take even longer. The Vexilar Edge 3 is a great liquid-crystal unit, running two simultaneous transducers, one at 107 kHz and the other at 400 kHz. This provides two different views on the full-color display to show both active, roaming fish and those sitting tight to structure. The unit is named the Edge because of its unique ability to display what's needed to keep the angler on a weed-line edge, where mid- to late-summer crappie take residence for long periods of time.

THE ROLES OF WIND AND CURRENT

Wind Considerations

When you're casting and trolling, wind direction and boat position must be carefully considered when it comes to catching crappie. North, east, south, or west wind direction isn't necessarily as relevant as the direction of the retrieve. Trolling with the wind regularly outproduces trolling into the wind; casting into the wind (which would then be retrieved with the wind) is similar.

If you're casting into the wind, it's important to adjust your presentation's weight in order to get it into the zone where crappie are present. However, the bait's action must also be considered, as too much weight can compromise this action. One useful technique that allows a light bait to fall faster under windy conditions is to cast and then place the rod tip just below the surface of the water after the bait has landed. This causes the line to lie down on the water's surface instead of billowing in the wind, which would cause the bait to move around in an unnatural manner instead of sinking.

Current Considerations

Practically any body of water will have some type of current during specific times of the year. Crappie can be affected both positively and negatively by current, and understanding its effects on fish behavior can help anglers use current to their advantage.

When people think of current, their first image often consists of a flowing river. Rivers are indeed excellent environments for crappie, but reservoirs and lakes are equally impacted by current, especially when caused by strong winds and precipitation runoff. In the heat of summer, areas of current typically have a lower water temperature than standing water, contain greater amounts of oxygen, and act as a liquid conveyor belt delivering a constant supply of food.

On many lakes visible current is shallow, within channels, and at the mouth of tributaries. Crappie won't remain in direct current for long but hide behind rocks and logs and near eddies. It is often advantageous to position the boat along the nearest primary drop-off. Fish sit along current breaklines that curb the strong current flow and wait for minnows and other forage species to float past.

Use a small jig, drop shot or Lindy, but increase the weight of the presentation substantially in accordance with the intensity of the current. A presentation that's too light will zip past the fish in a position that's too high for quality fish to chase. The bait must get down to the fish through the current, so it's imperative to utilize enough weight.

Another high-percentage area is open water. Many anglers falter when it comes to open water because they treat it all equally. Hearing the local fishing report state that crappie are currently suspended in thirty-five feet of water does not guarantee a waiting school as soon as the boat arrives at that depth. Sometimes areas hold fish for predictable reasons—such as forage, oxygen, cover, and water temperature—while other times fish are found in unusual areas for no apparent reason. Research for a fishing trip may include examining lake maps and GPS (Global Positioning System) units to find areas where the fish may be. But those predictions can prove incorrect, even with ample preparation. Using your electronics as your underwater eyes to first locate schools of crappie, and then trying to catch them, will greatly improve your odds … especially when it comes to roaming schools of deepwater crappie.

Mid- to Late-Summer Crappie Presentations

At the height of summer, a number of approaches can work, including trolling and vertical fishing over specific fish-holding structure.

Since crappie will be in deeper water than during earlier parts of the year, a number of effective techniques can be used. Water temperatures have now climbed to their peak and the fish are active, swimming actively to catch meals and burning calories quickly. Fast-moving baits can put a quick limit

of fish in the boat, but if the bait can display characteristics of an injured minnow, your catch rate will increase.

Casting for deepwater crappie is often most successful, since an angler can cover more territory without spooking any wary crappie that are positioned just beneath the surface. Trolling is another productive route when the fish have moved farther down the water column, especially during nonpeak times, when covering greater expanses can be beneficial. While vertically fishing for crappie produces far fewer fish, it can still prove useful, particularly when smaller schools of crappie lie in brush or standing timber, decreasing the likelihood of getting hung up on the wood.

Fall Crappie

Now water temperatures begin to decline with cool nights and north winds that make most people leave their boats in the garage. Fall can be an outstanding period for crappie, even when the weather is downright

Fall can be an outstanding period for crappie, even when the weather is downright dreadful. Scattered schools of crappie now become tighter, making it more difficult to find active fish, but delivering great results once such concentrations are located.

dreadful. Scattered schools of crappie now become tighter, making it more difficult to find active schools, but delivering great results once such schools are located. Deep weed edges along creek channels in reservoirs and adjacent to flats of medium depth often hold these closely grouped schools of crappie.

Fall Crappie Presentations

Using an electric trolling motor is a great advantage during the fall. Try pulling a $\frac{1}{16}$-ounce tube jig slowly over a weedy drop while systematically covering new water, stopping when a nice fish is caught in order to more thoroughly probe that spot.

Fall crappie holding on weedy drops may actively hit a jig on the fall, as it's jigged, or the moment it makes contact with the bottom. A good start is to cast the tube jig as far as possible, letting it sink all the way to the bottom on a slack line. Keep a close eye on the line, watching for any twitch that signals an attack from a hungry crappie. If the tube jig hits the bottom without incident, slowly drag your rod tip about eighteen inches to the side. Many times fall crappie follow a prospective meal to the bottom but have trouble locating it because of the slow downward travel. Dragging the jig gives the fish time to get to the bottom and visually pinpoint its meal by the slight movement. This dragging motion also simulates the movement of bottom-dwelling crustaceans, a favorite meal for a crappie.

Taking the time in fall to probe for crappies, rather than go waterfowling, can pay big dividends, as shown by this satisfied angler. RON ANLAUF

CHAPTER FOUR

Sunfish through the Seasons

Sunfish could arguably be credited with getting more kids involved with fishing than any other species. Their unabashed willingness to bite gets kids excited about accomplishing the feat of landing a fish. They're interesting to look at and fun to catch—a combination anglers of all ages can appreciate.

Because sunfish—specifically bluegill, green sunfish, and pumpkinseed—are so prolific and numerous, anglers often assume they can go out and immediately catch a large number of nice fish. But harsh reality sets in when the fish aren't where they were expected to be. Understanding seasonal location and how this can impact success is an important step in consistently catching more sunfish of any variety.

Sunfish, especially bull specimens like this, are certainly not just for kids. Who wouldn't want to hook into one like this?

Early-Spring Sunfish (Prespawn)

Following the disappearance of ice on northern lakes, sunfish remain fairly inactive for a few days as they adjust to the changes. The water begins to warm beneath the sun's direct beams, and sunfish slowly start to search for food that emerges in shallow bays and arms. Many believe that sunfish will establish residence in bays on the north side of lakes during the early-spring period. This is not always true, however, and is a theory based on the idea that these bays receive more sun exposure throughout the day. Taking the time to explore numerous bays and arms, with less focus on their compass orientation, will give you more insight to where the fish currently swim. In many situations, fish return to those areas from one year to the next, making it even easier to find active sunfish.

Early-Spring Sunfish Techniques

Sunfish are quite timid during the first several days after the ice departs. A small float with a miniature ice jig and waxworm, mealworm, or eurolarva is a superb choice for these early-season wanderers. The float should be extremely small so as not to spook the shallow fish, and a minimal amount of action should be provided. Thill's Shy Bite float is just the ticket due to its diminutive size, landing gently on the water above the waiting sunfish. Keep thinking small as you choose your line and hook as well. Two- to four-pound-test monofilament or fluorocarbon is ideal, and even though you have to be patient while reeling in fish, the result with light line is much better than heavier line, especially during this time of year.

Because light line, small baits, and a tiny float are being used, one might think the theme would continue when selecting a rod and reel. Actually it's quite the opposite. A longer rod, seven or eight feet, helps to launch the ultralight rig a greater distance from the boat or shoreline. Pairing a larger reel with the longer rod balances the combination, and the wider-diameter reel spool holds more line, reduces friction against the spool, and assists in propelling the bait through the air. And when one can make a long cast, the boat can be positioned farther away from targets, lessening the chance of startling the apprehensive sunfish.

Boat position is very important for locating a clear casting lane to structure and obstacle-free retrieval of bull bluegill. An anchor keeps a boat securely in place ... that is, until the wind blows, at which point the craft will simply pivot on the anchor rope and rotate to some degree. To eliminate this problem, use two anchors, one near the bow and another near the stern to minimize movement. Just be sure the anchor ropes aren't so tight that a series of waves produced by another boat in passing causes your vessel to rise and fall, lifting and dropping the anchors onto the bottom. This can create a plume of silt, sand, sediment, and weeds that may have a negative effect on the fish and your overall success in that area.

An alternative for achieving satisfactory boat position is to slowly slide along the surface, propelled by an electric trolling motor. The use of electric trolling motors has increased in popularity over the years, and the majority of fishing boats are equipped to sneak silently through the water. Noise isn't a significant factor with battery-powered electric motors, but the artificial current they produce at high thrust can stir up the bottom and alert fish of your presence, especially in very shallow water. To keep this to a minimum, use the trolling motor at its lowest possible setting to move your boat, while keeping the propeller at the highest feasible position beneath the surface.

Spawning Sunfish

Some of the secluded shallow bays that held large numbers of sunfish early in the spring are now becoming void of fish. This results from the development of weeds that often fill the area from top to bottom for the remainder of the summer and then die and decompose late in the fall and through the winter. When the water temperature rises into the high sixties, male sunfish begin creating nests in shallow main-lake areas near pencil reeds and cattails. They often use open areas and corners where the lakeshore turns sharply as well. Sparse cover is tolerated, but sunfish typically avoid spawning in areas with extremely thick growth. Though composed of numerous individual nests in close proximity to one another, a larger spawning colony is created and inhabited by many sunfish, each committed to its personal spawning bed.

Male sunfish create individual nests by fanning the bottom to remove fine sediment that may impede the eggs' development. The male then circles the nest, attempting to attract an interested female. The female approaches and deposits her eggs in the nest, often moving on to another nest to repeat this series of events. It's common for female sunfish to deposit eggs in multiple nests, and often more than one female will deposit their eggs in a single nest.

Once the female has left a total or portion of her 30,000-plus eggs, the male sunfish releases milt over them and remains to guard the nest. Periodically the male sunfish fans the bottom to circulate oxygenated water and prevent an increase of constrictive sediment. The eggs begin to hatch in a short period of time—one and a half to five days, depending on the water temperature. Although this incubation time is relatively short, the male sunfish remain true to the offspring for up to three weeks. After successfully providing care for the nest, the male sunfish has been known to replicate the process, creating a new spawning bed and coaxing another mate.

Sunfish may also spawn more than once over the course of spring through summer. Since the entire population of sunfish in a body of water won't spawn in one mass effort, it's not uncommon to encounter occupied nests on a single lake over a span of several weeks. The earliest spawning nests are formed in the shallowest water, while fish that reproduce later in the season may build nests in water to about 10 feet.

Spawning Sunfish Techniques

Catching spawning sunfish is generally a simple endeavor. The same jig and float presentation that was used for early-spring sunfish can also be used for spawning fish, and although it isn't mandatory to use such a superstealth approach, limiting terminal components and choosing small hooks and floats provide the best results. Now a slightly heavier line is applicable, with six-pound test being a good beginning. Ideally, more than one rod and reel should be available during a trip, with varying line weights on each outfit. That way you can have an ultralight outfit for those times when the fish simply don't seem enthusiastic about biting. Conversely, you can use a slightly heavier rod, of medium action with eight-pound-test line, when the fish are voracious and eager to eat nearly anything presented before them, especially when cattails, bulrushes, brush, lily pads, or pencil reeds act as a barrier to the spawning nest.

Casting accuracy is often critical in catching spawning sunfish. Because they are quite committed to their nests, it's important to position your bait directly overhead, as they won't meander very far from the region. Fortunately, though, anglers who might not have pinpoint casting accuracy can still catch a bunch of spawning sunfish, since they build nests very close together in large groups. Sometimes there are only a few inches between the cleaned-out depressions, so even though an errant cast may not land directly over a fish in sight, it may end up on top of one of the other nearby nests.

Heavier rods are often required when cattails, bulrushes, brush, lily pads, or pencil reeds act as a barrier to the spawning nests you're targeting.

A great way to learn about fish behavior is through observation, and this is particularly true about sunfish. Using a good quality pair of polarized sunglasses, observe the spawning sunfish for a short period of time, noting their mannerisms when another fish approaches. Intruders are chased away from the nest, and the highly protective sunfish will bite if the trespasser doesn't swim away fast enough. This can help to understand why getting spawning sunfish to bite your offering is rarely a complicated chore. However, vertical bait placement can be just as important as horizontal presentations. During other times of the year, a bait placed a few feet above a sunfish will often prompt it to approach, even in the middle of winter when the fish are quite lethargic. But during the spawning period, adult sunfish have to protect their eggs, which lie on the bottom of the lake. Therefore, the distance between your float and hook should be on the slightly lengthier side so that your bait is closer to the bottom, causing the aggressive sunfish to assume your bait is a nuisance. The fish will either attempt to move your bait away from the nest or simply swallow it in defense. Either way, your float relays the activity and you're in business.

A feathered jig or soft plastic body often works well beneath a balsawood float for spawning sunfish, but dressing the hook with some type of live bait or enhanced product will increase your catch rate substantially due to the presence of the natural scent and flavor. A favorite for spawning sunfish is a small leech because of its attractiveness and durability, remaining intact even after catching numerous fish.

Floats for Sunfish

Why use a float for spawning sunfish? Their focus is on what is below their bodies as they try to protect the susceptible eggs. Theoretically, one might assume that a simple jig that can fall to the bottom would work better. Well, many sunfish nesting sites are located right in the midst of vegetative or equally restrictive structure, and keeping the line at the same angle as the vertical weed growth decreases the chances of getting snagged. Casting a weighted jig without a float puts the bait and line at an angle that can easily intercept vertically oriented cover, making a snag more probable.

Different anglers prefer slip or spring floats, and there are pros and cons to each approach. A basic spring float, like the balsa-wood-bodied Thill American Classic, is high quality yet inexpensive and won't crack or take on water that could make it sink like a plastic float. The fluorescent-colored Thill Bubbl'Gum Bobber is another high-quality spring float available in colors that allow simple visual location.

Premium Thill Gold Medal floats, which are obtainable in many sizes and shapes for every situation imaginable, do not come with a spring mechanism for attachment to the line. Instead they are attached using nylon sleeves or, in the case of some models, a quick X-Change system that allows rapid replacement. This is a welcome feature when fishing varying species with a single rod-and-reel combination.

Many times anglers simply grab a random float and attach it to the line, paying little attention to the size of the bobber and how that is impacted by the weight of the hook, jig, or any attached lead shot. Instead the weight should be carefully calculated, tested, and then fine-tuned so that the very top of the float is barely exposed above the water's surface. This practice, called shotting, will decrease the amount of force required to pull the float under, thus avoiding detection by even the most discriminating sunfish.

Fish that grab a bait from below often swim upward, causing the float to lift and lie down on the surface. Realizing this is indicative of a fish, even though the float doesn't submerge, one should promptly set the hook. I have observed many anglers who simply wouldn't set the hook unless the bobber was completely underwater; there is no need to wait for this to occur. All fish are not identical in size or personality, and this is reflected in the way a bobber reacts when a fish grabs the bait. It may sink, rise, slide across the surface, descend half an inch and remain motionless, spin, or move in just about any other manner.

Postspawn Sunfish

After the spawn, sunfish move out to slightly deeper water, although they intermittently move from shallow to deep, and vice versa. Since their primary source of sustenance will come from insects and zooplankton, large schools of sunfish position just under the surface of the water. Sunfish feeding on surface fare create an audible "pop" as they open and close their mouths quickly on edible objects. During this period, fish congregate around shallow water structure in one to ten feet of water. Their preference for certain types of vegetative cover isn't as important as the presence of food, which at times may correlate with certain types of weed growth. Numerous varieties of insects hatch and emerge around specific weeds, and the sunfish gather in mass to feed. If you find a school of sunfish around a specific weed variety, try other places that have identical features when you decide to move. Discovery of more active fish in several different but structurally similar spots establishes a pattern and greatly reduces the amount of time required to locate active fish.

Postspawn Techniques

This period is a fly fisherman's dream. Since the fish are hyperfocused on insects and tiny surface creatures, many types of dry (surface) flies work well due to their realistic appearance and position at the top of the water column. The metabolic rate of sunfish has increased and food becomes a major focus, bridging the gap in response to live bait and artificial offerings.

You've probably heard the phrase "match the hatch," which refers to finding an artificial equivalent to the currently swarming insect variety. This isn't a procedure solely applicable to fly fishing; all anglers can benefit from the practice. Yet there will be times when a presentation that doesn't match the hatch, and in fact even seems quite absurd, catches more fish than any natural-looking offering. The only way to determine which bait will work best is to first go with what seems logical; if that doesn't work, begin experimenting. Many of the greatest ideas in the world of angling started out as mere trials by fishermen willing to test unique ideas, sometimes ridiculed by others for attempting such unconventional approaches.

Summer Sunfish

At this time of year, anglers can find numbers of nice-size sunfish in a variety of locations. Shallow water around docks, pencil reeds, bulrushes, brush, submergent weeds in medium depths, deepwater brush, logs, and green, leafy vegetation are all areas of interest to sunfish during the midsummer period. Often anglers fishing for other species such as walleye and bass encounter sunfish as a nuisance or pest, regularly attacking larger bass baits and nipping the ends from the live bait frequently utilized by walleye anglers.

Sunfish during the summer period occupy a variety of depths and structural elements, and finding larger fish can be more challenging compared to earlier in the year. Sunfish are now much more spread out, although they still travel in groups. Fortunately, when a school of nice-size fish is discovered, significant numbers are commonly caught. This is a good time to begin searching for larger fish in deeper water, where they generally receive less pressure.

Midsummer Sunfish Presentations

Deepwater brush and cabbage weeds discovered using marine electronics can easily be probed by swimming a small plastic jig. A $\frac{1}{32}$- or $\frac{1}{16}$-ounce jighead with a small plastic body, like the one-inch Little Joe Thumpin' Tail (a soft plastic bait with a C-shaped tail), delivers irresistible action when it swims. Another option is a miniature tube bait like the one-inch Little Joe Salty Tiny Tube. This hollow-bodied plastic bait has numerous tentacles that hang from the back, irresistibly undulating in the water and tempting the most stubborn panfish.

The most important thing to remember when rigging a soft plastic tail of any size, for any species, is that the artificial bait is threaded straight onto the shank of the hook. If the plastic bait isn't straight, the jig will helicopter on the fall and rotate on the retrieve, which amounts to twisted line and less attention from the fish.

Most anglers have spent a couple of minutes adjusting the eye, lip, or knot position on a crankbait to ensure it moves through the water correctly, without spinning or tracking to the right or left. But some of the same people forget to adequately attend to perfecting the performance of a tube bait, an oversight that is simple to correct. Since tubes come in sizes ranging from less than an inch to over eight inches, their purpose for use isn't limited to one species or relegated to representing one type of forage. A tube can emulate the antics of an injured minnow, an insect larva, and is also one of the best fleeing-crayfish simulators available. For any application, however, the situation calls for some attention to rigging.

The major focus of tuning a tube is to achieve true tracking, meaning that when the bait slides through the water while quickly retrieved, it runs straight without spinning or veering in any one direction. It's essentially the same goal you seek in a crankbait, although the process for achieving that end differs.

Many people think of tubes as baits to drag or hop, so why would an angler be so concerned with the way it swims through the water? First of all, fish see the bait as it hits the surface and falls, during which the bait is effectively swimming. That initial, descending impression is a high-percentage chance for a bite, and a spiraling tube doesn't look natural. Second, you'll quickly find that fish of all species will follow a well-tuned tube up to the boat when you least expect it. You might think that you're merely reeling in to cast once again, but keep an eye behind that bait. Third, if your tube spirals in the water, your line will be in knots by sunset if not sooner.

Tube baits can be threaded on a hook but can also be rigged with a

Using tubes on jigheads can be very effective.

jighead inserted into the hollow body of the bait, an option that hides the solid bulk from a fish so that it only feels the soft plastic of the tube, not the hard lead of a jighead. To do this, the jighead should be wet and then gently pushed into the tube before it's tied onto the angler's line.

Begin by selecting a hook long enough to clear the bottom of the tube's body to the point where the tentacles begin. A jighead/hook that is too short will create a bend in the bait, immediately impeding the desired action.

The most efficient way to insert the jighead into a tube is to moisten the head of the jig and push it into the hollow cavity of the tube from the bottom before the jighead is tied to the line. Make sure the jighead is as close to the top of the tube as possible; this is the first step in ensuring it's properly tuned. Then press firmly against the eye of the jighead, exposing

it to finally tie on the line; but before you secure a strong knot, be sure the jighead is straight inside the tube.

Your final alteration will be the tentacles. If any of the plastic strands are tangled or permanently curled, they should be straightened or pulled out. Attempt to center the hook among the tentacles, with the understanding that it's not necessary to count how many are on the right or left of the hook shank but that it should be approximately equal. Next, remove the tentacle nearest to your hook on both sides, providing more room for it to move freely and reducing the potential for a crooked jighead.

Now make a short cast and reel in rapidly. Though you probably won't utilize a constant cast-and-crank method while fishing the tube, this lets you easily monitor the action of the bait, determining the progress of the tuning process. If the tube spins, something still needs to be modified. A long day of using a tube that spins will leave you with a spool of tightly twisted line, leading to potential frustration. If all of these modifications haven't resulted in a straight-swimming tube, cut the line, pull out the jighead, and rotate the tube 180 degrees to try it all again.

Fishing a tube for sunfish can be done in various ways, but two that continually produce are dragging and hopping. Dragging a tube works wonderfully when fish are in a neutral feeding mood and want something that's moving slowly. Simply complete a full-length cast, and let your bait sink to the bottom. It's extremely important to watch your line at the point where it enters the water during the descent, as it can give you a visual cue when a fish bites; it also indicates the arrival of your bait on the bottom when excess line gathers on the surface.

After establishing bottom contact, gently pull your rod slowly to the side to dredge the bottom, essentially dragging it along. The key is to move it excruciatingly slowly, creating a slight disturbance of silt and sand. Since the hook on the miniature tube is exposed, it's quite possible that you'll become hung up in weeds, but this is a small price to pay for the increased likelihood of attracting some quality fish. Getting stuck in vegetation can actually catch help to catch some big panfish, since they're quite comfortable with plucking insect larvae and other water creatures from the surface of a weed stalk.

Hopping a tube is a good technique when the fish are actively feeding and want some flash and movement from their prey. Again, cast the tube and let it fall to the bottom or close to it. Now lift your rod tip sharply to

Opposite: One of the simplest and most effective means of putting together tubes and jigheads (top) is to merely insert the jig into the tube's hollow body (bottom).

make the tube quickly rise toward the surface, then drop the rod to allow the bait to fall again. Repeat the procedure while taking in line; you'll quickly find that aggressive sunfish will hit the tube on the fall, repeatedly surprising the angler as he lifts the rod tip for the next hop. The hopping action doesn't require a hookset-like yank to entice the fish but a short, quick-yet-gentle snap of the wrist to make the tube jig rise less than a foot.

Late-Summer/Fall Sunfish

As water temperatures begin to slowly descend and days become shorter, sunfish gradually disappear from the shallow water areas where they are so commonly seen earlier in the year. Docks and piers no longer house the curious fish as they migrate to deeper water for winter. (An unseasonably warm fall day can, however, bring them back toward shore for a day or two.)

Fall is a great time to catch some trophy sunfish, but locating interested fish of any size becomes much more difficult. Unlike the activity of bass, walleye, and northern pike, which increases substantially late into the fall as they indulge in preparation for a long winter, sunfish become increasingly lethargic. Deep, well-defined weed lines become the habitat of choice during this often-unpredictable period, although an Indian summer day can lure sunfish onto large, shallow weed flats adjacent to their cool-water refuge, positioning themselves just below the surface to enjoy the sun's warmth. A cool autumn wind the following day may push them deeper, back to the comfort of more stable water temperatures.

Late-Summer/Fall Techniques

The fishing pressure on lakes begins to lift, alleviating some of the stress produced by pleasure boaters, personal watercraft, and of course other fair-weather anglers. Sunfish will tend to gravitate toward a deeper residence.

A highly effective walleye presentation, the Lindy Rig can put big fall sunfish in the boat when some minor adaptations are made. When sunfish are biting short or aren't overly active, releasing line upon initial contact from a fish allows more time for the hook to make it into the fish's mouth. This is achieved by keeping the spinning reel's bail open while holding the line with your index finger.

Small leeches, angleworms, and nightcrawler halves are all great complements to a Lindy Rig modified for sunfish, but experiment with hook types. A #6 or #8 live-bait hook is barely visible when pierced through a leech or worm, but sometimes a subtle amount of extra visibility helps. Using a small wet fly or ice fly of little weight in place of the standard live-bait hook offers a slightly different look than what sunfish are used to during this time of year. Beads and spinners can also be added to the snell, but for fall sunfish a straightforward Lindy Rig without spinners works very well. A small chartreuse bead placed on the line above the hook can add just the right amount of visual attractant to make the live bait stand out.

CHAPTER FIVE

Perch through the Seasons

Anglers frequently encounter perch on massive flats and along steep drops that many deem "walleye country." Since perch are primary forage for walleye, the two often occupy the same neighborhood. Throughout the majority of the season, perch hold in deeper water, making it imperative to use a boat.

During the first year of life, young perch feed on varieties of zooplankton. After this period of growth and maturation, perch begin eating minnows in addition to plankton and small invertebrates. Anglers can capitalize on their affinity for minnows by using various small live-bait varieties and artificial baits and lures that represent minnows. These can include miniature crankbaits, spoons, and soft plastic baits in assorted shapes. As perch grow to adult size, crayfish are added as a food source. Individual large perch, occasionally of trophy proportion, rummage between the cracks between boulders and rubble looking for available crayfish. Small schools of perch are also known to "gang up" on an individual crayfish, picking the crustacean apart from different angles.

Early-Spring Perch

Because perch spawn soon after ice-out, the early spring period for this species is relatively short compared to sunfish and crappie. Ron Anlauf shares some insight regarding early-season perch.

"Unlike sunfish and crappie, whose earliest runs are mainly feeding forays that can last for up to a month, perch come in to feed and spawn in one fell swoop—it happens fast! The good news is the action can be extremely intense, and you can hit it big if you're in the right place at the right time."

Generally, perch remain in deep water or adjacent to it along edges of drop-offs and flats that are near deeper sanctuaries. But due to the dramatic environmental changes that take place during this period (quickly warming water from a more direct sun angle, longer periods of daylight, and the absence of ultraviolet ray–inhibiting ice and snow), perch move to shallow water, impelled by these environmental changes as well as their own biological clocks.

"Ice-out perch action can be absolutely phenomenal at times, and is really a matter of perfect timing," Anlauf adds. "The window of opportunity can slam shut quite quickly; a bit too soon or a little too late, and you could miss the whole thing. But if you're ready for it and take the time, you could easily find yourself in middle of a bay full of pole-bending jumbos, and it doesn't get much better than that."

Spawning Perch

Water temperatures that have warmed into the mid- to high forties now prompt male perch to move into shallow-water areas with rock, sand, and gravel as the primary substrate. Lack of heavy vegetation makes the spawning grounds that much more desirable. Not long after the male perch take temporary residence among the spawning area, female perch begin to arrive. Unlike crappie and sunfish, perch do not clear individual nests for their eggs. Instead a small number of males pursue an individual female, waiting patiently in the wings until she begins to lay her eggs. Once she begins to release the long, gelatinous string of eggs, a male approaches and releases his milt, fertilizing the approximately 25,000 eggs. The female then

immediately vacates the area, abandoning the handful of male perch that remain in the vicinity for a short time before they retreat to deep water. No adult perch stay to guard the eggs or greet the larval offspring as they emerge. (One interesting aspect of the spawn is that perch engage in the reproductive process throughout the night, a period of relative inactivity for the species during other seasonal phases.) The young perch feed upon zooplankton for much of their first year, and then graduate to small invertebrates, minnows, and crayfish. The mortality rate of the young perch is substantial, as numerous larger fish and bird species prey upon the vulnerable fish.

Opposite: Spring perch can provide a great day on the water. This one fell to a jig with a curly-tail grub. RON ANLAUF

Spawning Perch Techniques

Catching perch while they inhabit shallow spawning grounds is as much about timing as technique. Although perch can be caught throughout the handful of days while spawning takes place, their dedication to gaining nourishment takes a backseat to the reproductive process.

Since perch will be in close relation to the bottom, a bottom-dwelling presentation is going to be most effective. Because the fish will be occupied with spawning, positioning a bait directly in front of the perch is imperative. Reactionary bites during this period will outnumber strikes occurring from hunger.

Anlauf favors a light jig tipped with live bait when the fish are finicky and opts for artificials when perch are highly aggressive.

"The catching is what it's all about and is as pure as it can get," he observes. "Casting and pitching light jigs tipped with a plastic trailer and maybe a minnow is what we're really into, and is a great way to give your jigging skills a tune-up. A short cast to the edge of a weed bed, a close-in drop-off or breakline, or the middle of a bay will get you started, and all the aforementioned have the potential to hold active perch. Don't be afraid to pitch up into real shallow water, because you just never know the possibilities and don't want to overlook anything."

Apprehensive perch prefer a light meal that appeals to multiple senses, so live bait is preferable when activity levels are low, as it will appeal to the fish's smell, taste and lateral-line as well as its eyesight. Using a small live-bait hook, size 8 or 10, tied to the end of your line with a small split-shot positioned six to eighteen inches above it, is an excellent combination for spawning perch. Appropriately called a split-shot rig, this presentation works well paired with a small minnow and delicately cast to the spawning area where the perch await. When it hits the water, a few more feet of line should be released, allowing the rig to fall to the bottom. A leisurely drift or slow retrieve can be productive, as it gives the perch a longer opportunity to be lulled be the offering's many appealing attributes.

Postspawn and Early-Summer Perch

After establishing residence in deep water, perch often position themselves in the bottom third of the water column throughout the seasons, although a number of factors (especially food) will cause them to ascend. Good numbers of smaller perch will consistently inhabit shallow water, even at this time, but large perch prefer the deeper climes and only move shallow on occasion.

Very shallow ponds, like those found in the prairies of North and South Dakota, may not have deep refuge for perch; some of them may have a maximum depth of ten feet. Fortunately for the angler, these ponds are small enough that most if not all of the water body can be covered in a day. Keep moving and seeking productive areas; this approach will typically generate more fish than simply dropping the anchor and waiting in an area that you believe should produce. Pursue the fish; don't rely on them to discover you.

Postspawn and Early-Summer Perch Techniques

Immediately following the spawn, both male and female perch move out toward deeper water, congregating near primary and secondary drop-offs. If you're familiar with spawning areas, look for the nearest drop-off and begin fishing there, probing depths anywhere from fifteen to thirty-five feet. Nearby current is another attractant and can draw substantial numbers of hungry perch wanting to avoid strong flowage while waiting for food to wash past.

Once a school of perch has been located through the use of marine electronics, drop a jig, umbrella rig, or drop-shot rig right on top of the school. Often the fish will quickly jockey for position, attempting to be the

Aggressive perch will often be happy to grab a jig tipped with an artificial trailer. BILL LINDNER

first in line once the food falls to the bottom. Yet at other times lethargy is evident, and the once-aggressive school sits on the bottom practically motionless. Both activity levels can be observed using an underwater camera, but unfortunately the camera only offers evidence of fish behavior; it doesn't change it. At this point you're faced with a dilemma: Either change locations to find a different school of perch that may be more active, or spend some time trying to get the currently available fish to bite. Searching for additional schools can be a good bet, but two worthwhile options are first suggested that can impact perch behavior … and are quite simple.

First, using a slightly heavier jig, umbrella rig, or drop-shot rig, pound the presentation on the bottom. Doing this stirs up sediment and initially gets fish moving, either out of interest or annoyance. This is important because as the perch begin to move, the overall level of activity is already increased. The cloud created by disturbing the bottom may also have small amounts of food mixed in with the floating particles, surrounding the perch with edible microscopic meals.

The second option is downsizing. Changing to a supersmall jig or even an ice-fishing bait will often get those lethargic fish to bite. A larger meal may be of no interest at the time, but a miniscule offering may be all it takes to get inactive perch to open their mouths. Once a few fish from the school begin to engage in feeding activity, others will begin to follow suit.

Mid- to Late-Summer Perch

Networks of perch schools have now established residence on steep declines, humps, rocky reefs, middepth flats, protruding sandbars, and deep holes centered off main lake arms. Plenty of options exist for the savvy angler searching for midsummer jumbos, especially those familiar with procedures for catching walleye. Anlauf sheds some light on the distinction between perch and walleye tackle.

"The difference from walleye gear is the use of lighter line, with four-pound-test green monofilament being more applicable. The lighter line gives you more control and better feel with light jigs, and is less affected by the wind than the heavier stuff."

This becomes increasingly important as storms, cold fronts, and heat waves enter the region, all of which have the potential to produce high winds.

Mid- to Late-Summer Perch Presentations

Establishing productive patterns during the mid- to late-summer period sounds relatively simple, but even though water temperatures in deep water remain fairly constant, factors like wind, storms, fishing pressure, and boat activity can make perch change position from day to day.

One productive method for locating roaming or repositioned perch is trolling. Although you may be visualizing a 225-horsepower outboard pushing a boat at speeds uncommon for perch fishing, there are some alternatives. First of all, a high-horsepower engine can troll down to speeds more appropriate for catching panfish. The Mercury Verado, for example, has a system that allows the user to strategically dial in the appropriate RPM or speed to consistently keep the boat moving at your desired pace. Another option to reaching trolling speed with the main outboard is to attach one or two Drift Control drift socks to the stern of the boat, or one each to the starboard and port side front dock cleats. By doing so you'll not only decrease the travel speed but also increase the boat's stability, keeping the bow from bouncing uncontrollably in the waves produced by heavy winds.

A kicker motor is another alternative for trolling baits for perch. Typically 15 horsepower or less, gas-fueled kicker engines are equipped with specialized propellers that provide the power to push large watercraft at slow speeds. Newer models have a number of options that make their use even easier. Tilt and trim, electronic ignition, and four-stroke technology are just some of the available choices that make life easier. Four-strokes are a great choice for trolling with crankbaits and bottom-bouncers, and can be trolled down slow enough for jigging and rigging.

Another favorite propulsion system for these applications is the electric trolling motor. Mounted on the bow or transom, high-powered electric trolling motors are now so common that the boating industry and consumers consider them standard equipment. Many marine dealers prerig trolling motors on their boats to provide the consumer with a complete package that's ready to take to the lake.

The greatest complaint by anglers using an electric trolling motor for perch or any other species is lack of power. This only becomes an issue if the motor is too small for the boat or if the batteries are inferior. It's highly unusual to hear someone complain of having a trolling motor that has too much power. That's because all trolling motors can operate at a minimum setting that can be increased by minute degrees. The lowest possible setting, even on a very small craft, won't move the boat too fast. If ever in doubt regarding the proper-size trolling motor for a boat, go slightly larger than anticipated and avoid future disappointment.

The trolling methods that work best for mid- to late-summer perch can be either fast or slow, depending on fish activity—swiftly trolling a crankbait can put fish in the boat as well as slowly creeping along with a Lindy Rig or jig. Crankbaits cover greater expanses of water more efficiently, to locate active fish in less time, but rigging and jigging provide precision—an important attribute when working those minute discrepancies from one little spot to the next within an already inviting area.

Anglers actively searching for roaming perch with crankbaits can significantly increase their catch rate by incorporating scent and flavor enhancers on one of the front hooks. Walleye anglers commonly hang a small chunk of a (or an entire) nightcrawler on the hooks to generate more action. A piece of Berkley Gulp! accomplishes the same result. Perch go crazy over the combination, and anglers can capitalize on the effectiveness of integrating vibration, scent, flavor, and visual appeal.

Fall Perch

Having spent a substantial portion of the open-water season in relatively deep portions of a lake or reservoir, perch once again move into shallower regions. As certain species of minnows spawn in the fall, perch soon follow and capitalize on their susceptibility. Effective depths may range from a couple feet of water up to about ten feet, depending on where these hordes of minnows now reside.

Fall Perch Presentations

Anglers can capitalize on the perch's fondness for shallow-water fare by using the split-shot rig. This produced heavy perch earlier in the year during the spawn, but since these fish are no longer preoccupied with reproduction and have strapped on the feedbag, larger and more aggressive approaches can be used.

Live bait isn't necessary when perch are in high-feeding-activity mode. Small crankbaits prove very effective during this period, although the preferred style of crankbait may vary from lake to lake and from day to day. Casting will be the primary method for presentation, as trolling with an outboard in such shallow water can easily alarm fish. An electric motor can be more efficient, allowing the boat to move easily along shallow edges while the anglers hurl small crankbaits toward the shallows.

Crankbaits may be categorized in many different ways, but we'll begin by examining the means by which they situate themselves within the water column. Deciding on a floating, sinking, or neutral-weighted crankbait is an important decision to make even before getting on the water.

A floating crankbait remains at the surface until pulled through the water by retrieving it or trolling, and will dive to a certain depth based on the size and angle of its front plastic lip. Once the bait reaches the maximum diving depth, it stays at this level until the speed changes. When abruptly stopped, the crankbait's buoyancy causes it to float back toward the surface. This can be a great technique for many fish, but perch typically will only follow the bait back toward the surface for a very short distance. An erratic retrieve and pause does change the cadence of the crankbait, and doing so generates reactive strikes. Just remember to limit lengthy pauses while fishing for perch, and keep the crankbait lower in the water column.

A sinking crankbait immediately descends upon hitting the water, and it can be made to run at a known depth once the sink rate has been determined. To do this, pull two feet of line from the end of your rod tip. Now place the lure in the water and immediately position the rod tip so it barely touches the water's surface. As the bait plummets, carefully count the seconds to determine a rate of descent. If it takes two seconds to sink two feet, then it simply falls at an approximate rate of one foot per second. The plastic lip on the front of a sinking crankbait typically contributes more to its action than the overall diving depth does. And remember that if a sinking crankbait is stopped midretrieve, it will simply sink to a deeper depth.

Neutrally weighted crankbaits are a favorite for late-fall perch and possess a unique quality that the first two categories do not. When the retrieve of a neutrally weighted crankbait is halted, it neither rises nor descends but remains suspended at the current depth. This is a great attribute, especially when targeting fish that seem to snub every well-known bait and are neutral in activity. After cranking the lure down to the desired depth, temporarily pause the retrieve and wait several seconds. If nothing crushes the bait, gingerly twitch the crankbait and wait again. These intermittent, spastic movements make the neutrally weighted crankbait an easy target. One of the beauties to this presentation is that one can leave the crankbait, motionless and suspended, for as long as one desires.

Imitating the forage upon which the perch are feeding is a good start when choosing crankbait profile and color. Yet it can also pay off to break the rules now and then. When there's an abundance of identical baitfish, a presentation that stands out may actually perform better than identical simulations. Bright colors, awkward actions, and unique body styles are all options, and the only way one can determine their effectiveness is to give them a try.

Prime-Time Perch

Anglers worldwide commonly grapple with the question of when perch, or any other fish species, feed most actively and are easiest to catch. Although this can change periodically and without notice, understanding the relationship between physical characteristics and environmental changes can help you determine high-percentage times versus relatively unproductive periods. These factors will also impact the presentation you choose to catch perch. However, as with nearly every aspect of fishing, exceptions to the rules inevitably emerge.

First of all, "prime time" is influenced by numerous factors other than the calendar or a wristwatch, most of which relate to the physical attributes of perch. Since perch don't have overly acute eyesight, other perceptual senses are efficiently utilized in the feeding process. Blind spots in a fish's visual field, exacerbated by low water clarity, lack of ambient light, or obstructive weed growth, can be exploited by appealing to their other senses: taste, smell, feeling, and sound (detected by fish through the network of lateral-line nerves and an especially sensitive inner ear). Perch feel or hear prey within relatively close proximity, and then try to gain a position allowing visual confirmation.

Now think about the ramifications of having one of your own senses compromised. Human beings, when faced with this problem, adjust by placing more responsibility on their still-functional senses. This isn't something you'd contemplate or knowingly decide; it comes about instinctively, and the same can be said for fish.

How does this relate to determining prime time for catching perch? Since they remain relatively inactive throughout the night, partly due to their mediocre vision, first light brings a surge of activity. Lakes with minimal water clarity display heightened perch activity later in the morning as the sun's light intensity increases, penetrating the stained water. Clear bodies of water exhibit this increase in perch activity sooner, as the light reaches the depths that much more easily. Overcast conditions won't necessarily mean the fish won't bite, but the overall feeding intensity of the first-light period often diminishes, becoming spread out over the course of several hours. Numbers of quality perch can be coaxed to bite, but instead of using a presentation that looks realistic, brightly colored baits that scream to be seen work much better. Combining flash, vibration, flavor, scent, and auditory characteristics with the "colorful" theme draws accordingly more attention from perch.

TUBE TACTICS FOR PERCH

Many anglers don't realize that crayfish constitute a portion of a perch's diet. Baby crayfish can be swallowed whole, and slightly larger crayfish are sometimes bullied by one or more perch nipping at the crustacean's appendages. Instead of attempting to get the crayfish into their mouth, perch quickly bite the crustacean and retreat, avoiding its strong pincers and at the same time injuring it little by little, tossing it with sharp headshakes. Such crayfish try to escape, scuttling backward and gliding a few feet at a time by contracting their tail beneath their body. These motions allow the crayfish to move in reverse quite quickly, but the persistent perch will prevail unless the crayfish finds some cover.

If you've ever had the opportunity to watch a fish chase a crayfish in clear water, you may have noticed that if the crayfish intends to stay and fight, it adopts a posture with raised pincers. However, this stance often doesn't last long; the crayfish soon flutters it tail, tucks its pincers in front, and sails in reverse to attempt escape. It is worth observing that although the crayfish can walk both forward and in reverse, it can only swim backward.

Understanding these characteristics of crayfish behavior when trying to imitate one while angling can be beneficial. First of all, there are a number of artificial baits on the market that look identical to the outline of a crayfish, yet many of them have been created with the likeness of a crayfish in a defensive stance—claws extended out or up with a straight body. Perch will react to these the same way they react to the actual critter, by nipping at the appendages and biting the bait. They will not grab it with abandon, and will often miss contact with the hook.

An artificial fleeing-crayfish replica, which is far more likely to be engulfed by a perch, isn't as easy to locate in the tackle shops … that is, unless you know what to look for. You're actually searching for a specific action, not necessarily a bait produced from a crayfish mold. Nearly every tackle store has this, but anglers often mistake it for something entirely different. It's made of soft plastic, comes in practically any color and size, and looks like a squid. We are speaking of course about the soft plastic tube. It may look nothing like a crayfish at first, but when dragged on the bottom it, replicates both the profile and the movements of a runaway crayfish.

Since crayfish colors vary by body of water and geographic region, the color of tube you choose is important. You've already heard the phrase "match the hatch," referring to the coordination of color and size between the natural forage in the lake and the presentation you tie to the end of your line. Shades of brown and green are generally best in approximating a crayfish's hues.

Size is another characteristic that should be considered while purchasing tubes. Perch prefer smaller crayfish, so a tube in the 1- to 1½-inch category will get the best response, due in part to the probability that a perch will actually take the entire bait in its mouth instead of simply nipping at a portion of the tube.

Proportionally sized hooks should be chosen for rigging perch-size tubes. Small jigheads in the 1/64- to 1/16-ounce categories function ideally, but the hook size is equally important. A hook that is too long or large will look unnatural, and a hook that is too short or small can create a bend in the tube or make a hookup difficult.

Many anglers who use tubes insert the jighead by threading the tube on the hook similar to many other plastic baits, beginning on the side rather than the center of the top. By doing so, the jighead can be squeezed inside the tube. Unfortunately this creates a hole in the plastic, similar in size to the jighead itself, and it doesn't take long for the artificial bait to begin sliding off. Instead moisten the jighead and slide it inside the tube before you tie the tube to your line.

Now that you have the tube rigged up properly, let's examine how it should be worked. First, cast the bait out and immediately let it sink to the bottom. You'll know that it has hit bottom by keeping your rod at the ten or eleven o'clock position while carefully watching your line. Any line type will have a bend to it that remains fairly constant until the bait hits the bottom, at which point the line falls farther back toward the angler. If you see your line twitch or move to the side during this process, set the hook of course. Even a bite of significant force may not seem very notable, since your line and not the rod absorbs the shock. It's important to let the bait fall on a slack line, creating a purely vertical drop and attracting the fish from a distance, especially when fishing in clear water.

Once your tube hits the bottom, take up the slack and slowly drag the bait twelve to thirty inches. The key elements here are "slowly" and "drag." Remember, we're trying to make this look like a crayfish, and erratic jerks of the rod tip only make the bait move up higher in the water column and do somersaults, which won't look as natural. Once you've gradually pulled the bait the recommended distance, drop your rod tip back toward the bait and pause for a few seconds. This is often the moment when perch grab the bait, which resembles a live, escaping crayfish until it predictably drops once again to the bottom. Simply put, capitalize on the natural characteristics of crayfish when using tubes to target big perch.

CHAPTER SIX

Ice Fishing

The popularity of ice fishing has exploded over the past decade, with huge advancements made in the design of ice-fishing equipment. Gone are the days when anglers had to walk miles across the ice, chisel a hole by hand, and stare at their stiff wooden jig pole wondering if anything lurked in the water beneath.

Equipment

Today an ice-fishing trip is much easier, with increased comfort and mobility. Much of the equipment available is dedicated to hard-water angling and must therefore be considered separately from open-water applications.

There actually isn't a large amount of specialized equipment *required* to go ice fishing, but there's a plethora of specialized gear *available* for on-the-ice exploits. Striving for a hassle-free and enjoyable ice-fishing trip, certain accessories, even if they're not vital, increase the level of enjoyment whether or not fish are actually caught.

Ice Drills

One mandatory piece of equipment is simply an auger or chisel to bore through the ice to reach water. The best possible way to do this is with a gas or electric ice drill. These are available with various-size auger bits and motor sizes. Even though we're looking at fishing for panfish, an eight- to ten-inch hole works best, which is on the larger end of available bit sizes. This provides extra room to fight a fish without causing too much abrasion on your line from scraping on the sides of the ice, and it also gives the angler plenty of space for an electronics transducer.

Another consideration is the type of blade on the auger used to cut the hole. The bottom of a Jiffy ice drill has a ripper blade that can dig through ice quickly; and the additional grabber blades on the drill's point help to pull the blade downward. It's important to keep those blades sharp to achieve optimum cutting performance, so a hard protective cover should be attached when the blade's not in use. An ice auger bit should not be used to create holes in the earth and will not perform well after use as an ice chisel, even if the point of the ice drill appears able to chip away effectively at the lake's frozen surface.

There are few better ways to spend a winter day than panfishing through the ice. The rewards, as seen here, can be well worth it.

Electronics

Another piece of ice-fishing equipment that gives anglers a huge advantage is a flasher. Flasher sonar technology has been around for many years, and Vexilar, a marine electronics company based in Minneapolis, Minnesota, has been in the business since 1960. Its line of three-color flashers is well established for ice fishing today, clearly displaying the current depth, your bait, and fish that are present and at what depth. Just as important, the flashers won't show fish that aren't there. Understanding when to stay and when to move is important in all types of fishing but is especially relevant to ice fishing, since you are often waiting for fish to approach your bait. By using the real-time display on the Vexilar flasher, anglers can see the

Sonar units, particularly flashers, can be an indispensable part of the hard-water angler's equipment repertoire. CHIP LEER

absence or presence of fish and quickly determine if their techniques are working or not.

Additional Equipment

The final two large pieces of ice-fishing equipment deal with comfort and warmth. A portable ice shelter is a good idea for those days when staying inside sounds much more appealing than fishing on the open ice. And an ice shelter can only become warm with the assistance of the second item, a small propane heater. The flip-over type of portable shelter work best for those who want to stay as mobile as possible while ice fishing. It's very easy to move the entire shelter to another hole, and the flip-over canvas can be raised and lowered very quickly and easily.

Some other items that you'll need for ice fishing are an ice scoop to clear your fishing hole, strap-on ice cleats for traction while walking, ice picks for safety, and of course some rods and tackle.

Ice Rods

Ice-fishing rods for panfish typically measure from twenty to thirty inches and should be constructed of the same high-quality graphite you look for in an open-water rod. Spinning rods are the preferred choice for catching crappie, bluegill, and perch through the ice. The rod's action is just as important now as it is in the summer months—a rod that's too stiff won't allow you to feel a bite, while a rod that is too light could actually break while fighting a fish. When looking to purchase a rod, keep in mind that the products will differ in action and sensitivity, even though two rods from two different manufacturers may be labeled as "light action" or "medium" and are identical in length. Spend some time picking out an ice-fishing rod with a softer tip that telegraphs fish bites, combined with enough backbone so the rod doesn't bend all the way to the reel seat. Fig Rig's Ice-Fishing Series of rods is made with high-modulus graphite and has a seat that won't let your reel rotate on the rod handle—a welcome feature for anglers who have had a reel shift, or fall into the snow, during battle with a fish.

Ice Reels

Just as you would do when purchasing a reel for summer use, make sure the rod and reel match up well, recalling that for ice fishing we're pairing a spinning reel with a spinning rod. You're not going to be able to identify the balance of a rod and reel by sticking out your finger and letting the outfit teeter back and forth, waiting for it to even out. Balance such as that is appropriate to open-water combos, where efficient casting is critical. Here, casting is simply not part of the picture. Ice-fishing rod-and-reel balance refers more to the pairing of a like-size, quality reel to the rod. You want a reel that has ball bearings to aid in smooth retrieval, and the more ball bearings there are inside the reel, the better off you'll be. Since you won't be casting to the ice hole, a small reel is great—no need for oversize, distance-enhancing spools.

Line

Many companies have created line formulas specifically for ice fishing, considering the cold temperatures, abrasion from the ice, and need to camouflage the white of the snowpack. Three different types of line perform well for ice fishing in various situations. A personal favorite I use, actually rather uncommon among other ice anglers, is fluorocarbon because of its invisibility and non-water-absorptive qualities. This helps when you're fishing in extremely cold temperatures and constantly reeling in fish, since less water accumulates on your spool to freeze it up. This is not to say there isn't any ice buildup at all, but it is noticeably less compared to both monofilament and braid.

Braid is a good choice when you want a sharp response from your bait, like a jigging spoon. The contact with, and control you have over, your bait when using braid is unmatched due to its no-stretch quality. And the superthin diameter, although opaque, makes it hard for fish to see. Larger, tooth-wielding predators like northern pike are less likely to slice through braided line versus monofilament or fluorocarbon, making it an especially good choice when using techniques with a lot of flash (like jigging spoons or minnow baits for perch, or even with small baits) while in areas that are likely to have big fish nearby.

The Well-Stocked Icebox

The biggest mistake anglers make when transitioning from open-water presentations to ice fishing is trying to adapt their summer tackle for ice fishing. Many of the hooks and jigs used for all types of panfish during the summer months, although comparatively small in size to walleye, bass, and northern pike presentations, are still too big for winter panfish. The metabolic rate of your target species drops, and their interest in larger presentations declines. Instead of looking at crappie jigs in the $\frac{1}{16}$- and $\frac{1}{32}$-ounce categories, now you may be going as small as $\frac{1}{128}$ ounce. Of course if the fish are more active on any particular day, one can move toward larger sizes. (A good rule of thumb is to use much smaller baits for inactive fish and lean toward larger sizes for active fish.)

An ice fisherman will find many pieces of tackle that prove valuable in catching panfish. Some items to consider are teardrops, gnats, jigging spoons, jigging minnows, sinkers, plain hooks, and floats if desired. If you are using a sonar flasher, no float is needed to determine a bite. The

appearance of a fish joining together with your bait on the display and the subtle flex of your line indicate the need for a hookset.

Small lures made especially for ice fishing will perform better than their larger, open-water counterparts in the great majority of cases.

Vertical vs. Horizontal Baits

Depending on the design of the ice jig you choose, its profile will lie either vertical or horizontal. Pictured on the next page is a Lindy Frostee jig, a vertical bait, and a Lindy Genz Worm, a horizontal bait. These two

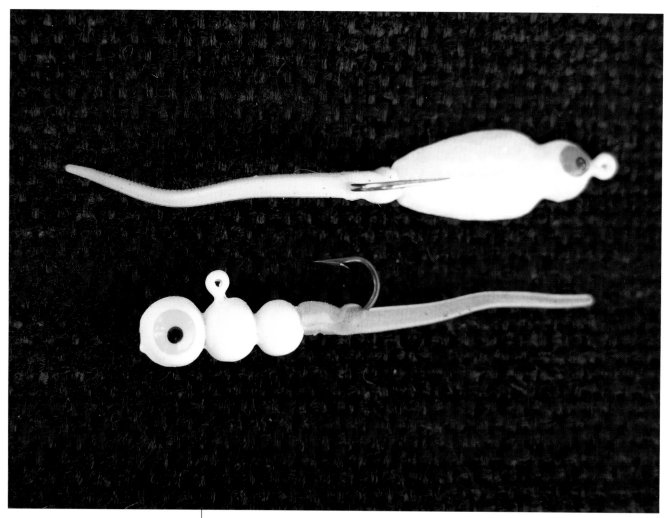

The Lindy Frostee jig (top) is a vertical bait; the Lindy Genz Worm (bottom) is a horizontal bait. Deciding how to rig the live-bait component to the hook depends on what kind of presentation you've chosen.

configurations should be carefully considered when attaching live bait or a plastic attractor. For instance, let's say you're planning to hook a minnow in a manner that allows it to swim and writhe naturally. To achieve this, it should sit parallel to the bottom. If you choose the Lindy Frostee jig, the minnow should be hooked through the back so that it remains parallel to the bottom. Use of the horizontally positioned Lindy Genz Bug permits an angler to hook the baitfish through the lips. Even though the hooking point differs for each jig, the desired outcome is very similar: a parallel, natural appearance of the minnow.

CHAPTER SEVEN

Crappie through the Ice

Location

Winter crappie can be found in a number of areas, depending on the specific body of water. Some lakes have a larger population of nomadic fish that follow schools of baitfish around, suspending in water twenty-five to sixty feet deep. Others contain more fish that relate directly to vegetation and steep depth changes, hiding within the weed stalks to ambush small minnows or wandering above the vegetation in search of water insects and plankton.

Typically, deepwater fish can be found just off main lake points and outside small bays and coves. Probing the deep water adjacent to shallower weeds flats can also be productive for suspended crappie.

Weed-relating crappie sit in much shallower water, since vegetation typically doesn't grow very deep due to the water's absorption of sunlight. Ultraviolet rays can reach deeper in very clear water as opposed to stained water, but the presence of ice and snow makes it even more difficult for light to help with weed growth. Most weeds experience prolific periods of growth and maturation throughout the summer and begin to die late in the

fall. Environmental factors during winter don't encourage much growth, but leafy green weeds can still be found, with the healthiest vegetation present in shallow to middepths. The search for winter crappie begins in eight to eighteen feet of water containing the proper elements for weed fish: Flats with steep outer drop-offs, variations along straight vegetative walls, and weed humps and points are generally productive regions for crappie.

Ice anglers in search of winter crappie will find greater success by planning their quest while referencing a map. Advances in paper map design and the development of astonishing mapping capabilities for GPS units allow for scientific exploration of a specific body of water, even if you reside several states away.

On the Internet, Google maps (google.com) show detailed pictures using aerial photographs, displaying a summer view of your favorite lake. Jutting points, sandbars, humps, and dense surface vegetation are all easily identifiable. This may help in determining possible winter fish locations, even though the photos are from a warmer season.

Paper topographical maps are easy to use and often include information such as water clarity, available species, bottom content, weed-line depth, average size per species, and stocking information. Some even include suggestions of areas to fish and what baits perform consistently. Even though there are other high-tech options for navigation and fish location, a paper map remains the most economical.

A GPS unit is a larger investment, but it gives you the ability to see your actual position in relation to a map. This becomes a great asset when attempting to locate offshore structures such as humps, creek channels, and weed lines. And when a school of fish is discovered, a mere push of a button will save the position for easy return in the future.

After referencing a map, cut up the lake into sections. Don't look at the entire body of water as a whole, but instead examine small sections by their distinguishing characteristics; each section will be easier to decipher than the whole body at once. Visualize each bay as a separate small lake, and find a couple bays that have structural elements you can proficiently cover. After you catch whatever species you're after, take note of the distinctive features that held the fish in that region and look for other areas that are similar.

One difficulty in locating winter crappie is mobility. During the summer months anglers can gradually move their watercraft using an

Opposite: Crappie days through the ice, in the dead of winter. What could be better? JEREMY ANDERSON

Success in ice fishing depends in some measure on the compromise you reach between the inherent stationary qualities of the pastime versus your ability to move to new areas as needed. A well-organized ATV or snowmobile aids in that balance.

electric trolling motor, drift with the wind, or even anchor and use a series of fan-casts to effectively cover the fishing area around the boat. When ice fishing, you have limited areas of coverage and are trying to get the fish to approach your bait.

Once you arrive at the spot you've previously determined to have potential, begin drilling holes in a section perhaps twenty yards by twenty yards, pacing intervals of five to fifteen steps between holes. Spend a minute or three at each hole, watching your electronics closely to determine the presence or absence of fish. Look for features that may set one group of holes apart from the rest, such as an isolated patch of weeds or a quick rise or drop. Now change your focus from looking at the larger area to an area the size of a one-car garage, systematically eliminating the unproductive portions. Once this has been accomplished, refine your area to one the size of your vehicle. As you can see, the purpose is to reduce the overall fishing

The sight desired by every wintertime panfisher: a nice fish coming through the ice hole.

area by eliminating the least-productive zones to concentrate on the prime fishing area. This is how to discover a small, highly productive region that should prompt you to save the waypoint on your GPS.

Deepwater Crappie Considerations

Discovering suspended schools of deepwater crappie is like finding a hot slot machine in a casino: There's the surreal feel of continually beating the odds, followed by the emptiness experienced when you stay a couple hours after the success has ended. Deepwater crappie can be addicting, and the unknown odds can keep you coming back night after night (when the majority of anglers try their hand at cashing in on the schools of wandering fish). But why deep water instead of shallow?

Once you discover a school of crappie suspended in deeper water under the ice, the results can be more than satisfying.

Opposite: The right equipment, the right location, the right time, and the right techniques make up a recipe for success.

Deepwater crappie are there for one main reason: food. Schools of baitfish can concentrate populations of crappie, even though the former's security is somewhat compromised compared to a residence within shallow-water vegetation.

The greatest advantage for the angler when targeting deepwater crappie is a flasher. Because deepwater crappie often suspend, a flasher is imperative to positioning your bait within the zone where crappie will acquire their target and attack it: directly above their heads. Crappie rarely descend to approach a presentation, but dangle a minnow or strategically hooked waxworm slightly above their station in the water column, shaking it gently rather than violently ripping the bait, and you'll get results.

Crappie cannot effectively see downward, so a bait consistently positioned within a few feet of the bottom will catch the occasional deep-dwelling fish but will go unnoticed by those cruising the upper three-quarters of the water column.

A flasher will typically reveal schools of active crappie suspended in the upper quarter of the water column, meaning that in forty feet of water the primary feeding fish will be only ten feet below the surface. You can see how easily anglers lacking ice electronics could sit on the ice for hours with their bait positioned below the point where active crappie would be feeding—and assume that the fish simply weren't biting that day. To sum things up: Get a flasher.

Winter Crappie Presentations

Since you will be targeting crappie situated in two distinct locales—shallow weeds and deep water—a number of approaches can produce. Some presentations will apply both shallow and deep, while others work better in one of the two. In states that allow the use of more than one rod, a couple of different presentations can be used to determine which one produces better; it also gives the fish more choice—an important factor when crappie are especially finicky.

An all-time favorite for winter crappie anglers is the simple float-and-minnow combination. Similar to that used for open-water crappie, this presentation in slightly smaller format will fool panfish in most ice-fishing

Small spoons and jigs account for a disproportionate share of crappie caught through the ice.

situations. Despite its effectiveness, however, there are times when it may be contraindicated. The changeable variables of a float/minnow combination greatly impact its effectiveness. Line weight and composition; jig size, color, and shape; and even the size of the float can positively or negatively influence crappie. Generally speaking, smaller is better (as is often true in ice fishing). As the fish become increasingly active, the size and overall activity of a presentation should increase, but otherwise, think small.

Spoon-Feeding Winter Crappie

Jigging spoons are a common choice for winter walleye, northerns, and bass, but many anglers mistakenly pass on jigging spoons for crappie, even though a jigging spoon often makes sense for winter crappie under a number of circumstances. Since anglers are confined to an overall vertical approach and it's imperative to bring in active fish from a distance, a jigging spoon should be one of your first choices. A jigging spoon is larger than most other presentations you'll use for crappie through the ice, but the extra flash and vibration can bring the fish in from a distance. Tiny spoons in the $\frac{1}{32}$- to $\frac{1}{8}$-ounce sizes are what crappie respond to best. Some anglers change out the spoon's treble hook for a small single hook, but whichever format you choose, the attractor you add to the hook is more important. Waxworms, eurolarva, spikes, mealworms, small minnows, or even a minnow head are all great live-bait choices.

If you choose to use one of the worm/larva varieties, hook the bait just one time near the end. The bait should hang straight down from the hook. Now lower the spoon into the water and position it slightly above any fish targets you see on your flasher. If none are currently present, experiment with various depths, working from the bottom up. The action you want to give a jigging spoon for crappie is much different from what you would provide for a northern pike, lake trout, or walleye. Instead of jerking, ripping, and hopping the spoon, gently shake your rod continually. Your goal is to get the hook to dance, jiggle, and flit. The body of the jigging spoon should move very little, allowing the worm to emulate a struggling minnow, the worm flashing like it's a writhing minnow's belly.

To accomplish this you'll need a fast-action rod; otherwise the weight of the jigging spoon will bend your rod tip, making the spoon move farther vertically than it should. The medium-weight Fig Rig Ice-Fishing Series rod has an action that most anglers would consider for walleye fishing, but the fast tip makes it a great choice for shaking a jigging spoon for crappie. And shaking the spoon is really what you'll be doing, concentrating the constant movement of your rod tip to an area of about an inch.

A small minnow attached to the jigging spoon by hooking it through the lips will work as well, but utilizing just the minnow head works even better. The key to using a minnow head for crappie or any other species is to remove the head from the body by pinching it off, rather than cutting it with a knife.

Another option is to attach a soft plastic tail to the jigging spoon, allowing an angler to reduce the time it takes to rebait a hook. (And since we're talking about ice fishing, the extra time your hands remain in your gloves proves beneficial over the course of an ice-fishing trip.) Plastic tails, such as the Lindy Munchies Tiny Tails, have been created specifically for ice fishing. The slender, flagella-like wisps of scented and flavored plastic last much longer than conventional live bait. The combination of a jigging spoon with the Lindy Munchies Tiny Tails is a deadly duo for winter crappie.

Other choices for synthetically simulating live bait include Berkley's Power Bait maggots and Berkley Gulp! maggots. These two live-bait look-alikes disperse high concentrations of natural scent, simulating the presence of live bait with greater longevity.

Three, two, one ... fish! This approach is an energy-intensive but very productive means of maximizing results.

Double-Duty Crappie: The Three, Two, One Approach

Maximizing one's ability to catch fish is why anglers continually refine their techniques, gathering input from fellow fishermen, reading about fishing, keeping logs with pertinent information—all to plan and help them catch more fish. On the ice, the three, two, one approach is an easy way to increase catch rates for practically any species. The basic idea involves three holes, two ice fishing rods, and one flasher.

In states where more than one line may be used per individual angler, pairing two ice-fishing rods and reels with different presentations provides the angler with more flexibility to discover winter crappie's preference. Flasher owners have the ability to pull double duty with their electronics: By drilling three holes in a line with only a few inches between them, the transducer for the flasher can be placed in the center hole; the display will show the two separate baits dropped down simultaneously in the two outer holes. If the water is shallow, the holes will need to be positioned very close to one another and may not clearly show both baits. But as you move into deeper water, the transducer can see increasingly larger areas. The standard transducer angle for a Vexilar flasher is twelve degrees, which means in ten feet of water you can see an area approximately 2.2 feet wide. However, this is the distance you would see if your gain was turned to the maximum, which it is not when you're fishing, so the actual area is slightly less. In twenty feet of water an angler can see approximately 4.3 feet; in thirty feet he can see about 6.3 feet. So in theory you could place the outer two holes of your three-hole sequence more than twelve feet apart if you're fishing in thirty-foot depths. There are of course certain pragmatic problems that prevent holes this far apart from being simultaneously fished. Staying within the realm of reality, spacing the holes about six inches apart works out well. Because the transducer is kept in the middle hole, you have few worries about getting tangled up with the transducer cable when you hook a slab crappie.

A popular add-on to the Vexilar flashers is the LED FlexLight for night fishing, which won't have much impact on your flasher's battery life at all. It consists of three superbright LEDs, and the draw is measured in milliamps, a fraction of what conventional light sources use for energy and only one-tenth of the power your flasher requires. And for anglers who want to use the "three hole, two rod, one flasher" technique, two FlexLights

Proper use of some baits' luminescent qualities can make a significant difference in attracting fish.

can be mounted to the Vexilar Propack II, giving you illumination for both of your prime fishing holes.

Setting the Mood: Utilizing Glow as a Subtle Attractor

I remember buying a jar of luminescent paint when I was ten years old, thinking that my most recent and partially assembled model car could use a paint job. After swabbing the doors and hood, I decided to put a few strokes of the glow-in-the-dark paint on some of my favorite fishing lures. And a few weeks later, when I spotted a battery-powered camera flash for only 50 cents at the local church rummage sale, I knew it was meant to be.

Now things are a little easier. It seems that nearly every tackle manufacturer offers a line of baits with radiant glow potential, in a variety of color options ranging from the original off-white hue to extremes of blue, green, and red. There's no need to find your inner artist, since it's simple to purchase a prepainted glow jig.

After dark is presumably the ideal time to capitalize on these baits' ability to be seen against a dark background. But people often overlook the subtle feature of a glow-bait used midday. The extreme contrast after dark can sometimes actually be too much. Think of all the subtleties anglers pay attention to while using other baits throughout the year. Changing factory rings and hooks on crankbaits to create the perfect combination, trimming skirts on jigs and spinnerbaits, bending hooks for just the right angle, but never contemplating controlling the light and color emitted by a glow-bait for ice fishing. Remember, in pitch-black situations it takes less light to create a drastic appearance. Think of turning on a flashlight outdoors in the middle of a clear sunny day, on a cloudy day, and in the middle of the night. The same light and intensity are visually perceived in three very different manners due to the ambient light available in the immediate environment.

Now consider the same concept from the perspective of a fish beneath the ice. For most of the winter their underwater world is dark, or at least much darker than the open-water season. Snow sitting on the ice doesn't allow much light to penetrate the water, and as the snow gets deeper, even less light comes through. A bright sunny day provides the best opportunity to utilize the effectiveness of a glow-bait, even in clear water. The soft glow of a jig may be the answer to trigger a bite from a finicky spectator.

Water clarity becomes another important factor when considering the use of glow-baits. Humans can see quite a distance on land, but even the keen-eyed walleye has decreased visual acuity in stained water. Offering a luminescent bait that's been held below a Lindy Tazer for a few seconds will give fish of all species a simple means to locate your presentation ... even in the middle of the day.

CHAPTER EIGHT

Sunfish through the Ice

Winter sunfish, specifically bluegill, aren't difficult to find during the winter months and are one of the more active freshwater species when ice time arrives. Targeting respectable keepers creates more of a challenge, and locating—much less catching—a trophy fish of a pound or more can be a real accomplishment.

Strategies for finding hard-water bluegills are akin to those for deep, summer sunfish. Since ice continually thickens throughout the bulk of the season in most locations, a three-foot-deep area can constrict to less than a foot over the course of a winter, and bluegill won't inhabit the area. Even though you can effectively catch bluegill in a foot of water or less during certain times of the year, winter is not a prime season for doing so. However, the same areas where you will find deepwater sunfish, particularly during the latter part of the open-water season, will remain profitable through the ice. Remember, these are areas that have well-defined weed edges, isolated deepwater vegetative bundles (separate or in combination with other structure), and open areas where sunfish can roam and find abundant food.

Huge Bluegills: The Equation for Location

Bluegills through the ice. This one took a well-presented ice spoon.

Ever caught a truly huge bluegill? I'm not talking about a twelve-ouncer someone claims is upwards of a pound, but dinner plate–size bruisers.

Finding gargantuan bluegills can definitely be tough. On any given body of water, the smaller sunfish will greatly outnumber the larger fish. Even the population of respectable half-pound fish seems enormous compared to the number of substantially larger females. An eight-ounce fish will be between four and five years old, while a one-pounder may be similar in age but different in genetic makeup. Considering that the typical lifespan of a bluegill is only five to six years, the likelihood of encountering a trophy-size sunfish is minute.

But there is good news to fuel your desire. Certain lakes are more apt to support larger panfish than others, and several factors can contribute to the possibility of a trophy's presence.

Opposite: Some winter days are characterized by short warming trends, without compromising the ice's integrity. The big fish don't seem to mind, either.

Relieve the Pressure

Obviously, lakes that have less fishing pressure offer a better chance for a trophy, since the sunfish are less likely to encounter humans as a predator. But the aquatic ecosystem must also possess stability, without an overabundance of any one species. Stable aquatic environments have natural predators, which make for stronger, hardier prey populations; posses a variety of cover and spawning areas; and have adequate to high amounts of natural forage. The maximum depth should be enough that winterkill caused by lack of oxygen available in the water is minimal.

Bigger Is Better

Large bodies of water have greater trophy potential due to abundant natural forage, allowing fish to sate their appetites at will. Lakes with light fishing pressure compared to large bodies of water may sometimes appear contradictory at first, but they often share promising features.

Leech Lake in northern Minnesota is a good example of this. It is a massive body of water with substantial fishing pressure, but the majority of anglers seek walleye, perch, and muskie. Bluegills are often ignored by those looking for the thrill of big or numerous fish. The ice and access points certainly have the appearance of plowed superhighways, but certain areas are actually void of pressure. Just remember to use caution when exploring track-free territory with fresh snow.

Genetic Mathematics

A major factor influencing your chances of catching a large 'gill is genetics. Catching one huge bluegill on a body of water can be a fluke, but catching a few often means the presence of larger groups and genetically superior subgroups. There may be offspring capable of growing to one or two pounds, but currently only weigh a portion of that. Should you feel bad about keeping a respectable few for the frying pan? No, but be reasonable in numbers and highly discriminatory in size. Ask yourself the following: Do you really need twenty to make a meal, or will ten suffice? Can it wait

When keeping big sunfish, be reasonable in numbers and highly discriminating in size. Releasing large sunfish gives future year classes an opportunity to possess similar genetics.

until another day when you're on another lake with a large population of panfish that could benefit from an increased harvest?

Shallow-Water Considerations

Many farm ponds and large shallow flats on natural lakes involve water less than twelve feet deep—and harbor fish that are eager to bite. Certain factors and events can substantially affect the number of fish you catch throughout your shallow-water outing. Developing an understanding, and even simply gaining awareness, of the following four factors will contribute to a hot frying pan at the end of the day.

Drilling Holes

Focusing on the technique used to manipulate an auger through the ice isn't typically a priority for most anglers, aside from striving for a somewhat

Cutting that ice hole requires some thought. Artificial current created when the auger breaks through the ice can agitate sediment and affect the fish to varying degrees, especially in shallow water. AARON PAPPAS

straight entrance into the water, but shallow situations require a refined approach. Consider the impact of your auger bit after it breaks through the bottom of the ice and enters the water. Some people increase the rotational speed, push the auger head down as far as possible, and then pull the entire bit out of the hole in an attempt to flush the slush out of the newly drilled hole. Two events take place when this technique is employed: First, as the rapidly spinning auger bit enters the water, an artificial current is created. This can have either a positive or negative effect on the fish in the area. If the auger moves deeply into the water column, it may also cause some disturbance of the vegetation and sediment. Again, this may be either positive or negative as to how it affects fish attitude. Some species may be drawn to a slight disruption of the bottom, but most will avoid the major chaos of chopped weeds and a sea of mud.

Visual Fields

Due to the biology and structure of a fish's eye, shallow water limits its ability to visually locate food sources. This causes them to become increasingly nomadic. Small schools of sunfish travel in search of sustenance, taking cues from one another as to which direction may lead

SECRET SOCIETY

To some anglers, locating huge bluegills is like striking oil or finding a valuable jewel. To others it is a place to catch a mess of big bluegills for dinner. Be cautious about revealing the secrets of your fishing hole. During the soft-water period a boat can, by chance, encounter a good area and fish ineffectively in any one category of location and presentation or incorrect depth, speed, or boat position and miss out on active fish. But the trails on the ice are easy to find, and even a little information can lead another angler to your iced-over holes. Leave your bragging for another day, and remember that by giving up too much information, you may be giving up your ability to encounter these fish again.

It's even more important to be discreet about publicizing honey holes in winter—they can be found all too easily by other anglers traveling over the ice. This one took a small jig from an unnamed location.

them to a food source. The angler is directly impacted by this rapidly relocating behavior. An area may appear to be devoid of fish until your flasher suddenly lights up and there's a steady stream of action for a minute … then nothing. Even the time it takes to simply remove the hook from a fish can cause a school to continue its search in another direction. Keeping a second rod nearby that's baited and ready to put to use can limit the lag time and put more fish on the ice.

Working toward decreasing the amount of time it takes for the fish to approach your bait is another topic to consider. Presentations that utilize large, flashy baits are more likely to draw fish in from a distance, even if that particular bait is unlikely to be eaten. For example, a wooden spearing decoy rapidly circling the ice hole may attract bluegill from long range, even though they physically could not eat it. But dropping a small jig and larva into the scene at the right moment can then prompt a feeding frenzy.

The Effectiveness of Your Electronics

Understanding the capabilities of your electronics is extremely important when targeting shallow-water fish. Knowing the transducer's cone angle is important, since you may not see a fish that is possible to catch. Shallow water not only limits a fish's ability to see, it also limits an angler's ability to "see" using his electronics.

The most popular units on the ice, Vexilar flashers, have three available transducer cone angles: nine, twelve, and nineteen. In extremely shallow water situations, even a wide cone angle won't cover a large area, but the flasher nevertheless remains a necessity in determining fish presence and response to your bait. A nine-degree transducer reveals slightly less than one foot horizontally in five feet of water; at the other end of the spectrum, a nineteen-degree transducer covers approximately 1.7 feet horizontally in the same depth. It may not sound like a lot, but identifying the presence of fish is the first step toward catching them, and the Vexilar remains equally advantageous for both shallow and deep water.

Pressure

Well-known shallow-water areas will have fishing pressure even when the bite is slow. On-ice activity affects the fish much more in shallow water than in very deep water, and constant vehicle traffic and auger protrusions also definitely impact fish activity under the ice. Exploring areas that have structural elements that are similar to highly productive community holes without the presence of anglers may bring you to untouched populations of active fish.

Fishing the pressured areas while the activity is light is another useful approach. Early mornings are a great opportunity—the fish have had the entire night to recover, and first light is often an inviting time for the fish to feed.

Shallow water not only limits a fish's ability to see, it restricts an angler's ability to "see" using electronics.

Frost-Shot Sunfish

Anglers searching for panfish have always had to carefully experiment on each ice outing to find the perfect bait for the day, seeking the proper amount of flash and vibration paired with subtlety and finesse. An interesting presentation that combines both is the Frost-Shot rig.

The Frost-Shot is attached to your line the same way a drop shot is configured for summer use. First, fasten a Lindy Genz Bug to three-pound-test Berkley Micro Ice line using a Palomar knot, leaving a twelve-inch tag end to tie on a large Lindy Frostee Spoon with the treble hook removed. You can experiment on the distance between the Genz Bug and

the Frostee Spoon, but it won't take long to find out that this rigging option catches fish.

The Frost-Shot works so well due to a couple factors: First of all it combines flash and vibration, produced from the Frostee Spoon, with the subtlety and finesse of the Genz Bug. It attracts panfish with the spoon's flash, and when the fish arrive, they can easily detect the Genz Bug hovering above them.

The rig performs better than a dropper rig in which the spoon is tied in line above and the smaller jig is attached at the bottom of the main line. The jig's movements are isolated, and the angler has much more control over its motion. Since the jig is tied on with the Palomar knot, every time the rod tip is jiggled, the Genz Bug moves in a hinged, rocking manner that works extremely well for undulating a waxworm, eurolarva, or soft plastic Lindy Munchies Tiny Tail as an artificial alternative.

Although this rig is created with similarities to a drop-shot rig, it's fished much differently. Drop-shot rigs were designed for bass fishing during the open-water season, although slight adaptations have been made to make them a great choice for fish of all species. The use of a drop-shot rig is specific: Cast the presentation to an area and let the weight sit on the bottom while gingerly lifting the rod tip to make the soft plastic bait dance and shake, without ever bringing the bait closer to the boat. It essentially allows an angler to fish vertically in a horizontal situation (casting from a boat).

While ice fishing, the angler is vertical fishing of necessity, so there is no need to position a weight on the bottom to keep a bait from moving horizontally. But ice fishing, even with the advancements made to increase mobility, requires anglers to attract fish toward the bait from the immediate vicinity. If that range can be increased and fish approach from an even greater distance, then the chance of catching more and bigger fish is greatly increased.

One scenario in which the Frost-Shot works great is during low-light conditions. Dusk and after dark call for more flash, as does the presence of muddy or stained water. The flash and vibration of the Frost-Shot calls the fish in, and when you hit the Frostee's Techni-Glo finish with a Tazer, the luminescent qualities simply add to its attraction.

Another prime scenario is in shallow water. Since fish don't have the same field of vision in very shallow situations, the Frost-Shot rig is much easier for fish to hear and feel, bringing them close.

Opposite: The Frost-Shot rig can be very effective on wintertime sunfish through the ice.

The last scenario that calls for a Frost-Shot is clear water. Even though fish can see much farther in clear water, we're still trying to increase the area from which we're attracting fish. In clear water this area increases dramatically, and the combination of flash, vibration, subtlety, and finesse provided by the Frost-Shot rig performs admirably.

CHAPTER NINE

Perch through the Ice

Walleye anglers can tell you about jumbo perch, as they often encounter the active species in shared areas where walleye lurk. Rock, sand, boulder, gravel, rubble ... pretty much any type of hard bottom accommodates perch, and attentive anglers who have noted those areas during the open-water season have a head start on a successful day of perch angling through the ice. Yet these walleye zones with a hard substrate aren't the only areas that attract perch, especially in winter. Weeds also appeal to perch: Flats and weedy drops in close proximity to deep water serve a perch, and an astute angler, well.

Finding a school of perch while angling through the ice requires an elevated level of patience, especially when Mother Nature is at her worst. But even under ideal conditions, locating active perch is much more difficult on the ice compared to open-water angling from a boat. During the open-water seasons, a boat rigged with functional electronics can browse through acres of aquatic environment in a short time, offering a fluid, continuous view of what's available beneath the transducer. During winter, however, a hole must be drilled and then the transducer placed in the hole, giving you a picture of what's directly beneath. Instead of gathering information

continuously, as you would in a boat, the angler is now "freckling" the area. It's similar to a painter covering a house by stippling—using only pinhead-size dots to cover the structure's exterior instead of painting with long, broad strokes. It's not hard to imagine which technique takes far less time and leaves fewer areas without coverage.

Arriving at a precise, predetermined area is one aspect of ice fishing that can be elusive. A paper map can offer some good general information, but pinpointing a spot still takes a substantial amount of time. A handheld GPS can be priceless when it comes to returning to previous locations. Pair it with the capabilities of a mapping chip, and now the icon on the display shows exactly where you stand in relation to depth contours, another invaluable resource. If you're fortunate enough to own or have access to a handheld GPS, you'll quickly find that although you can direct your efforts to a very specific spot, there will still be some work to do in drilling holes to find the "sweet spot" where the fish and baitfish are currently sitting in relation to, say, a twenty-foot contour, main lake hump, or saddle.

Pouring a small amount of water on the surface of clear ice and placing your transducer in the puddle offers an accurate view below without requiring an augered hole. Placing the transducer inside a small plastic bag filled with water and securing it with a twist-tie makes things even easier—now the transducer immersed in the sandwich bag can be set down and a reading established instantly. You will, however, still lack continuity in reading bottom contours because you cannot simply drag the transducer across the ice. It must be picked up and gently set down again to keep the transducer upright so that it reads straight down instead of at an angle. Even though the transducer appears to be a durable part of your electronics, it's actually one of the most delicate. The interior is composed of a crystal that can become damaged if carelessly tossed around or otherwise abused. If the crystal retains its integrity, your electronics will function

Opposite: The yellow perch—plentiful, energetic, and tasty—is a definite staple of the ice angler.

Electronics are essential for proficiently locating fish below the ice, no matter which species you hope to catch.

properly, but a damaged transducer will undoubtedly create problems and result in the need for a replacement.

Techniques for Winter Perch

The action that perch desire from a bait is much different from what attracts sunfish or crappie, although they are frequently caught in the same areas as other panfish. Instead of throbbing or pulsating actions, perch are attracted to sudden, highly animated movements. Flash, vibration, and sound all positively influence a perch to bite, and hyperactive anglers have found the key to creating good responses from fish in active, neutral, or even negative moods.

Spoon-Feeding Jumbo Perch

The jigging spoon is probably the most popular winter bait for perch. Small spoons tipped with a waxworm, eurolarva, mealworm, whole (or partial) minnows, or spikes are generally very attractive to winter perch. Worms can be hung from the hooks, threaded in gobs, or artistically arranged to provide an appealing profile. Small, whole minnows give off an entirely different scent and taste, while a minnow head on the hook can get even wary perch to strike. As described earlier, instead of removing the head of the minnow with a knife or scissors, pinch it off. This disperses even more scent into the water, often driving perch wild. If you cringe at the thought of decapitating a minnow, and waxworms don't turn you on, a soft plastic tail can be satisfactory.

Drastic Plastic

For years anglers thought plastic baits without a live-bait add-on wouldn't catch fish under the ice. The idea of artificially fooling winter panfish was simply written off by most fishermen. One of the primary reasons soft plastic baits never produced compared to live bait was the fact that many anglers would tie on the same jigs, tails, and lures they used to catch panfish in the summer. Remember, the metabolism and overall activity level of a fish decrease substantially in winter, especially in the northern regions, prompting companies to create specialized hooks, line, even rods and reels, catering to the particular requirements of ice fishing. Over the past couple of years, some clever ice anglers decided that instead of adapting soft plastic open-water baits to ice fishing, it was time to create artificial baits specifically for ice fishing, like Lindy's Munchies Tiny Tails.

Jigging Spoon Technique

Vibrant, flashy, dancing jigging spoons call perch to your fishing area from a distance and can quickly become an angler's "go to" presentation once proficiency has been attained. You can't simply tie on a jigging spoon, drop it down the hole, and expect perch to arrive en masse like southerly migrating waterfowl. The technique you use to give that spoon action is just as important as the hooks—you won't catch fish without it.

Shaking Remember that perch are attracted to motion. After dropping the jigging spoon tipped with live bait or an artificial tail, constantly shake the rod tip, moving it within a very confined area (less than an inch). This causes the treble hook and live bait (or artificial attractor) to flutter, but without moving the main body of the spoon much.

Adding a small but colorful plastic or metal attractor to the split ring of the treble hook further increases the appeal; and worms, minnows, Lindy Tiny Tails, or prominently scent- and flavor-enhanced Berkley Gulp! maggots can provide just the right amount of color, texture, and flavor.

Jigging Lowering the jigging spoon to a position close to the bottom, snap your wrist to make the spoon jump six to twelve inches. Aggressive perch will try to destroy the spoon while you're jigging it, but they are more likely to strike as you take a break from the motion. A brief pause is the perch's window of opportunity to assault your jigging spoon. The actual jigging process attracts the fish—the pause provokes the strike.

The Lindy Flyer Jigging Spoon reacts uniquely to jigging motions. Instead of a gliding rise and descent, it does a somersault at the height of its ascent, which winter perch seem to go for. The internal rattle chamber creates an audible chime, further enhancing its attractiveness.

A-Bomb

When a school of perch is present but inactive, sometimes the only option is to instigate a feeding frenzy. The closely schooling perch have definite influences on one another, and when one becomes aggressive, it can prompt a chain reaction. The A-Bomb technique does just that, and even though the process goes against traditional thinking (slowing down and jigging less vigorously), it can result in a significant increase in feeding activity.

Drop a small to medium-size jigging spoon to within a foot of the bottom, and gently shake it for a few seconds. While continuing to shake the spoon, slowly begin to raise the presentation by lifting your arm—not by turning the reel handle—and bring it to several feet above the bottom. Now proceed to quickly drop your rod tip to touch the surface of the water in the ice hole. The spoon in turn has dropped and made contact with the bottom, creating a small cloud of silt and debris that stirs up bottom-lying microorganisms. The jigging spoon appears to be injured and susceptible, giving the perch a chance for an easy meal. Let the spoon lie there for a few seconds, then give it one sharp jerk, letting it fall to the bottom to rest once more. Finally, lift the jigging spoon to a height within a foot of the bottom, and continue to shake it gently.

Often a few perch will approach the spoon the first time it falls to the bottom but will keenly observe the motionless bait instead of grabbing it. The next hop off the bottom often draws a strike, and catching a couple of perch by "bombing" the bottom quickly excites others into activity.

Keep in mind that the premise behind the A-Bomb technique is to create a minor disturbance of the bottom, not a major catastrophe. Generating a muddy mess that stretches through the water column and spans several feet will deter perch instead of encouraging them to bite.

Jumbos on Chubbies

Jumbo perch dwelling under the ice love minnows. It's no secret that crappie and fathead minnows writhing naturally on an ice jig, or a minnow head draped on the hook of a dancing jigging spoon, put big perch on the ice. But reaching into the minnow bucket when temperatures plunge below zero isn't much fun, especially when the perch are on a frenzy and bait requires frequent replacement.

A bridge between live and artificial bait is the Salmo Chubby Darter, a minnow lure designed for vertical jigging. The Chubby Darter vibrates irresistibly when jigged and enticingly rocks when gently shaken. Big perch love the Chubby Darter and aren't apprehensive about eating the artificial bait. The smallest size is most productive for huge perch.

The Salmo Chubby Darter is an excellent option while vertical jigging for yellow perch.

Dropper Rigs

Because activity draws perch into the immediate vicinity, a jigging spoon or vertical jigging lure is like an underwater flashing neon sign. But if the fish approach and decide it's simply too much of a meal, the initial attraction becomes moot. This is where the dropper rig comes in. Start by tying on an attractive jigging spoon, and remove the treble hook. Now attach a three- to eight-inch length of fishing line to the spoon where the hook had been. Finally, tie a small ice fly to the end of the line, dressing it with a eurolarva, waxworm, mealworm, minnow head, Lindy Munchies Tiny Tail, or Berkley Gulp! maggot.

Adding sound can further enhance the presentation's appeal. This is easy to accomplish by using a Lindy Rattl'r Spoon as the visual attractor from which the dropper line dangles. As the name implies, it has the added element of sound to help bring in those curious fish.

All the previously mentioned jigging spoon techniques can produce with a dropper rig, but the conditions at hand will dictate the appropriate and most useful approach—more often than not, some experimentation will be necessary.

Back to the Drawing Board

When the extreme flash and action fail to put perch in the bucket, go back to the basic tenets of panfishing. When in doubt, decrease the size of your bait and give the fish supersmall morsels. A tiny ice jig, paired with one or two larvae and delicately jiggled, is still one of the best presentations for winter perch. The throbbing worms are still a perch favorite—and may be just what you need on your next trip to the lake.

Good luck!

Caring for and Cleaning Your Catch

Anglers utilize different techniques for cleaning fish, particularly panfish. Some prefer to scale the fish, keeping the skin intact with the meat. Others fillet their catch, eliminating the bones that can be troublesome at the dinner table. Both techniques, along with many other hybrid methods, are acceptable as long as the end result is pleasing to the chef and table guests.

After first catching a decent-size fish for the table, place it in a live well, inside a cooler lined with ice, or on a stringer. The goal is to keep the fish alive as long as possible or immediately cool it on ice. Once you arrive home, fish should be cleaned promptly. Time can have a negative effect on the integrity of the meat, so minimize the chances for spoilage by attending to your catch as soon as you get home. Many anglers simply use newspaper laid out over a table or countertop, which aids in the cleanup process. (Check state regulations if fish are to be transported after the cleaning process. Some states have precise requirements, and proactive steps need to be taken while cleaning your fish, such as leaving the skin intact for easy identification by fish and game officers.)

Selecting a good fillet knife and keeping it sharp are imperative to cleaning fish effectively. A good general rule is to use a smaller knife for smaller fish and a larger knife for larger fish. For most panfish a four-inch blade works well, but some larger crappie might be cleaned more easily with a six-inch version.

One of the most popular ways to clean panfish is to fillet them, resulting in a bone-free slab of meat that can easily be coated and fried, marinated and baked, poached, or delicately grilled. To fillet panfish, begin by making a vertical incision just posterior to the gill covering (figure 1). Begin at the

Figure 1

top of the fish and cut down until you feel the blade hit bone, then make an incision down to the belly. Be careful not to cut too deep around the head, which could puncture organs and allow unwanted fluids to touch the meat.

Next rotate the fish 180 degrees and make a long cut from the top of the head to a few inches past the end of the dorsal fin, from the head of the fish to the tail (figure 2). The knife blade should be parallel to the cutting board while following this procedure. At this point the fillet knife can be pushed through to the bottom of the fish and brought toward the tail. It's important to keep the knife blade parallel to the dorsal fin as it's extended through the fish so as to keep the blade flat against the spine.

Figure 2

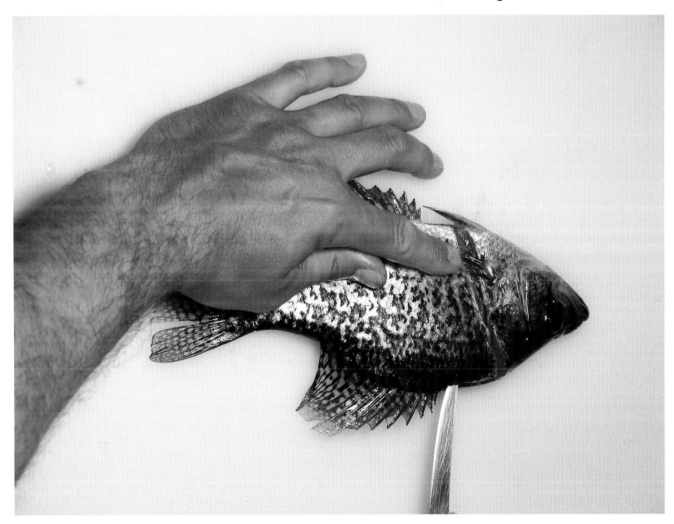

Now return to the starting point near the head, and begin to continually cut away the meat from the body of the fish (figure 3). The anatomical configuration of all panfish is similar: They are essentially a flat plane except for the outward bulge of the ribcage. The spine can be used as a guide. Now carefully navigating over the ribcage and cutting through the belly, create a single piece of meat that hinges at the tail and can simply flop over flat against the cutting board. Some people leave the fillet and skin attached to the fish while they separate the meat from the skin, while others cut through the small area near the tail.

Figure 3

To separate the meat and skin, place the flank scale side down and begin cutting directly between the meat and skin starting at the narrow end. Carefully keep the blade flat, parallel to the table. Slide the knife back and forth at an angle and cut against the skin, not through it (figure 4).

The very last cut you will make removes the pin bones. These tiny bones are nearly unnoticeable in very small bluegill and perch after cooking, but are evident on larger panfish. Examine the fillet closely and you will notice a faint, reddish line situated in the center. Cut on both sides of the line four-fifths of the way to the skinny end and discard the thin strip (figure 5).

Following this step, the remaining piece of meat should go into a bowl of clean cold water while you fillet the other fish. Dispose of the skin and scales.

After cleaning your entire catch, thoroughly wash each fillet in cold water. Now you are ready to prepare a meal with your bounty of fresh fillets or stash them in the freezer for another day.

Figure 4

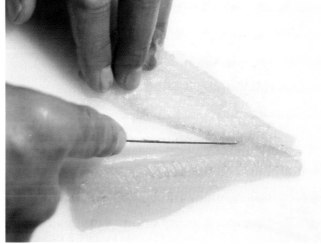

Figure 5

INDEX

Italicized page numbers refer to photos

Northern Minnesota writer, professional angler, and fishing guide Jason Durham spends every possible minute on the water. He has always been fascinated with all types of fish, possibly because he grew up in a community of 350 people with nearly one hundred accessible lakes within a ten-mile radius.

Durham started his business, Go Fish! Guide Service, at the age of fifteen, and he continues this entrepreneurial endeavor to this day. He admits that, in the beginning, his dad had to launch the boat as he was too young to drive.

Today Durham spends his summers guiding and his winters teaching school. With bachelor's and Master's degrees in education, Durham teaches kindergarten. His classroom reflects his passion for fishing: a large aquarium containing various freshwater fish sits in the center, providing fun and knowledge to the students.

Durham delivers seminars on species-oriented angling at boat shows and sporting goods stores, educating others so they can catch more and bigger fish. He also dedicates large portions of time to educating youth anglers through seminars, clinics, and on-the-water instruction. "Granting a child the opportunity to go fishing is wonderful, but witnessing a youngster emerge as a conservationist and steward of the outdoors is a gift."

Durham's second book in this series is titled *Pro Tactics: Ice Fishing*.